Comprehensive Christian Coach Handbook

Essential Guide to Spirit-Led Coaching and Business Success

By Leelo Bush, Ph.D.

Beautiful Life International, LLC

Cape Coral, Florida© Copyright 2017 – Leelo Bush, Ph.D.

All rights reserved. This book is protected by the copyright laws of the United States of America. This book may not be printed or photo copied for commercial gain. Use for personal or group studies is encouraged and allowed.

All scripture quotations, unless otherwise indicated, are taken from the Amplified Bible, Copyright © 1954, 1958, 1962, 1964, 1965, 1987 by The Lockman Foundation. Used by permission.

Scripture quotations marked "KJV" are taken from the *King James Version* of the Bible with permission. Scripture quotations marked "NIV" are taken from the *New International Version* with permission. Scripture quotations marked "Message" are taken from The Message Bible with permission. Verbatim Scripture quotations are set in italicized type.

Beautiful Life International, LLC – publisher
Cape Coral, FL 33904

www.beautifullifeinternational.com

All rights reserved.

ISBN: 978-0-692-85363-4

What People Are Saying About
Leelo Bush, PhD

PCCCA has greatly impacted my life because Dr. Leelo Bush is an amazing woman of God, which is quite evident in everything she teaches and stands for. As a Minister myself, I prayed for more wisdom in my counseling style, so that I could impact lives even more. God led me to (Christian life coach training at) PCCCA, where I learned greatly from their (Premier) one-to-one style of coach training. I am a better person with a deeper understanding of my clients' needs and how to help them since I graduated from PCCCA. Also, because of my training with PCCCA my practice has grown tremendously. I admire you and thank you Dr. Leelo Bush for the influence and impact you had on my life. May God bless you always as you continue to touch lives.
~ Linda Christine Scarlett, Washington State
Certified Christian Life Coach, Counselor, Author

I am very excited about Dr. Leelo's certification programs. I am currently enrolled in the Christian Life Coach course and soon will be enrolled in the Christian Counselor Certification. After many months of thoroughly researching various Christian programs, Dr. Leelo Bush and her Professional Christian Coaching & Counseling Academy (PCCCA), won hands down. Dr. Bush's professionalism, genuineness, and knowledge of the appropriate subject matter far exceeds that of any other program I looked into. In addition, her

support system which includes her emails, her Facebook pages and articles/blogs provide necessary and valuable information for success. To be able to see Christ's light shining bright within her inspires me as a new trainee to complete these courses and further set up my own coaching business. I am grateful and extremely blessed to be a part of this program and looking forward to completion. I highly recommend PCCCA to anyone considering enrollment. Thank you.
~ *Elena L. Beal, Colorado*

PCCCA is an awesome academy of excellence that offers training for those who know they are called to help others. The training has increased my level of excellence personally and has given me the ability to build a successful coaching practice for women.
~ *Angela Tezano, Louisiana*
Certified Christian Life Coach

Praise God! I had been told there were no "authentic" Christian – meaning biblically-correct life coaching courses. But something made me keep searching the web. I had almost given up when I found PCCCA. Dr. Leelo Bush's courses are all based on the truth of God's word and she does not compromise to please the secular world. You can TRUST that the training you receive from Dr. Leelo is the best available because it agrees with scripture and it's very practical. She created Spirit-led Christian Life Coaching and it has been an honor and privilege to study under her. I will be back for more training.
~ *Georgette-Lynn Osmond, Canada*

It is with great joy and much appreciation that I am sharing my experience with PCCCA and Dr. Leelo Bush. When God called me to be a Christian Life Coach I honestly was uncertain if this profession existed. Much to my delight, the internet provided me with a few resources. There were several people from schools and academy's that I spoke with and knew immediately that PCCCA was the one God chose for me. It had all the right credentials: Love for God, his children and a genuine Christian Heart. I received my certification after learning much about Christian Life Coaching. Then the hard part came with the realization that I would be transitioning into a new life and profession. I wanted even more of the coaching-specific techniques and skills to successfully start my own practice even though I had some background in business ownership

already. I recognized the need to gain assistance from a Christian Life Coach. Dr. Leelo Bush generously gave me the love, support, ideas, techniques and resources necessary to continue in God's perfect calling. May anyone reading this be blessed with the same opportunities!
~ *Jenny Grace Morris, Missouri*
Master Christian Life Coach with numerous additional PCCCA certifications

When I was doing my "homework" searching for a Christian Life Coach Program, I was seriously considering one particular program, but I felt the Holy Spirit guiding me instead to PCCCA. Now I know why. PCCCA is completely in line with my Christian values and my belief that the Word of God is sufficient. Thank you PCCCA, for not compromising to align with the world's view.
~ *Linda Noel, Pennsylvania*

In 2008 I had to stop working outside the home and care for my ill father full-time. It was then I began taking Dr. Bush's courses to keep my mind sharp and give me more skills to earn extra income in ministry after Dad passes. I really enjoyed working one-to-one with my trainer/mentor coach, Todd Miller in the Premier CCLC course at PCCCA) and I have enjoyed taking other courses through Dr. Bush. I am so thankful for her flexibility with me and support as I care for my father and do my studies. I admire and respect Dr. Bush's pursuit of continual learning and development of programs to serve God and others. My goal is to hone my skills, continually grow and learn and one day be a Master Coach utilizing my education and the experiential training given to me by God to help others for His glory.
~ *Gordon Rogers, Illinois*
Certified Graduate of Multiple PCCCA Courses

When I decided to acquire my coaching certification, I was adamant about enrolling in a purely Christian training program. I wanted no part of any New Age nuances that sometimes parade around as Christian values. I researched several programs before deciding on the Professional Christian Coaching and Counseling Academy (PCCCA). The training was academically rigorous and the certification requirements let you know that you had earned that certification. I got my money's worth and I am proud to display my PCCCA certifications on my website. Thank you, Dr. Bush, for

the hard work you clearly poured into this program. Thank you for strong accountability and thank you for invaluable lifetime lessons that go far beyond certification.
~ *Linda F Williams, MSW, Michigan*
Certified Professional Life Coach / Certified Christian Life Coach

Dr. Leelo Bush is truly a pillar within God's Kingdom to impart instruction through the integration of wisdom, Bible principles for living, deliverance and with an outcome for empowerment. The curriculum is quite comprehensive yet very clear for the student in pursuit of becoming a Certified Coach or for the person seeking to grow to dimensions God has purposed for them. I have truly enjoyed and gained much insight sitting under Dr. Bush. Her passion and demonstrative integrity is the reason I believe the Holy Spirit led me to PCCCA. I have met others who studied elsewhere and I must say, the many concepts covered through PCCCA are not available where they studied. The content is rich and allows the newly Certified Coach to step out with much confidence in God. I am also grateful for the bits of advice and encouragement from her mini-training topics that provide great mentoring for us as students and graduates. Dr. Bush, I Praise God for you and thank you for allowing Him to use you in this capacity. God Bless you.
~ *Rose Campbell, Florida*

The contents of the Stress Relief course were easy to follow and very well organized. My goal was to learn how to better help others and your course even included how to hold sessions for individuals and groups. I also learned how to create corporate stress management programs. I began coaching and already have paying clients. It will take some time to build my practice so I can leave my other profession, but I know exactly what I need to do to succeed. By the way, your support team is great and I always receive the answers I need in a timely manner. Thank you for making this training available for us online. Once I get my certification, my wife will be taking the Christian counselor course so we can fulfill our dream of working together to help our church and community.
~ *C. J. Smith, Pennsylvania*

To God be all the glory for great things He has done! Since the fall of 2003, I had visited the PCCCA website watching it evolve, praying, comparing the PCCCA training program to that of other schools,

and contemplating whether or not to enroll. Well God's timing is perfect timing and on March 16, 2006, the Lord said "yes" and released me to enroll in this anointed program. From my initial call with my trainer, I knew that this was a divine connection ... My experience at PCCCA was truly a blessing empowering me to prosper. I have learned skills that have positively impacted my life. I will never be the same and I am excited about my ability to help others reach their God-given potential and to fulfill their earthly purpose. "A man's mind plans his way, but the Lord directs his steps and makes them sure" - Proverbs 16:9. Heavenly Father, I thank You for directing my steps to PCCCA and making them sure.
~ *Sheri Cooks, New Jersey*
Certified Christian Life Coach

Attending PCCCA has been a blessing to me. The contents of the course is thought-provoking and purpose-driven. This course has allowed me to examine myself and ask God to remove anything in me that would prevent me from becoming an effective Professional Christian Life Coach. Dr. Leelo Bush, emphasizes that prayer is the key ingredient and to let the Holy Spirit guide us. I have begun to pray more for guidance and direction. I have become a better listener and have learned to manage my time, so that I am efficient and productive. I believe this course produces life-changing results for future coaches if a person truly desires to do the will of Christ. Thank you Dr. Leelo Bush!
~ *Gloria Ford-Mims, Georgia*

Over the past year and half, I have had the opportunity of receiving training and certification through PCCCA as a Certified Christian Life Coach, a Joy Restoration™ Coach, and a Stress Relief Coach, as well as being privileged to attend Dr. Bush's Barefoot Mastermind™ seminar and Advanced Coaching course. I am now a candidate to become a Master Christian Life Coach. When I began this training, I knew that I had God's calling on my life, but I had no direction and few skills to bless others. Through this training, I have learned to listen intentionally before I speak. As I have learned to listen, I have also learned to consider others' perspectives both in my personal life as well as with my clients. Thanks to Dr. Leelo Bush and my training with PCCCA, I am now blessed professionally with my own coaching business and personally with an ability to be compassionate, productive, and filled with joy. Longtime friends

and acquaintances have all commented that they can see the Spirit's peace flowing through me, even amid significant challenges, because through PCCCA, I have learned specific skills to place God first and allow Him to guide my journey.
~ **Wendy Mueller, North Carolina**
Certified Graduate of Multiple PCCCA Courses

Several years ago I was praying about my life choices and career. After a few days I was led to contact Dr. Bush regarding the Life Coaching Certification. Taking this course was a great eye-opener. I realized that I was being called to become a Christian Life Coach. Because of the information I learned, my life has made a total change. One of the benefits of her classes is that they are bible-based. They inspired me to change my thought patterns by meditating on the word of God. I have been blessed to use the information to lead the Men's Ministry group in my local church. I was also inspired to write a book on family issues. One of the things I have learned to is let the Holy Spirit flow through me. Thank you Dr. Bush.
~ *Marvel Jenkins, Texas*
Certified Professional Life Coach / Certified Christian Life Coach

I recently took the training course on Joy Restoration Coaching from the Professional Christian Coaching and Counseling Academy and I was greatly blessed, both by the material I studied, as well as by the resources that were made available to me through the Academy. This course has greatly enhanced my professional Coaching skills to help those struggling with life issues to move from painful to joyful living, and I highly recommend it for anyone who wants to help others overcome their grief and live a happier life.
~ *Renato Amato, Italy*
Certified Joy Restoration Coach / Certified Christian Grief Coach

My name is Dr. AudreyAnn Moses. I am a PCCCA Certified Christian Life Coach. I graduated from PCCCA in 2010 and have been blessed beyond measure since then. God has opened many doors for me because I now have a Christian coaching credential in addition to my previous psychology / counseling background. Clients benefit from my ability to identify with their description of issues they see and feel, while at the same time maintaining my position as a coach, not a psychologist, which helps them to identify their goals and objectives for their life. My background in Christian coaching also has benefited me as a consultant, workshop facilitator and keynote speaker. I am so grateful for the Christian coaching approach I learned while a student with PCCCA as well as the information I received through the emails and newsletters I continue to receive as an alumnus. Thank you very much for the assistance received throughout the years. PCCCA is a blessing from God. Continue the good work and God will continue to bless the school. I know He is continually blessing me and my business.

~ **Dr. AudreyAnn Moses, *South Carolina***
Certified Christian Life Coach - CCLC

The training I received from PCCCA has been extremely beneficial to my life. My family has been the primary beneficiary of the training, and they continue to benefit as we grow individually and as a unit. As a Family Systems Coach, clients, friends and people I meet for the first time generally admire and ask what's our secret to communication and keeping our family together. We understand that the family is one of God's four institutions and that there are Biblical guidelines and protocols to follow on a personal level. Coupled with the relevant training PCCCA provided for me, I help families acquire a wholesome desire to achieve the same benefits and results.

~ **Marina Edwards/*Trinidad and Tobago***
Certified Joy Restoration Coach / Certified Christian Grief Coach

Completing the PCCCA's Christian Life Coach Certification training was a wonderful experience for me and definitely enriched my life. I found the course to be very comprehensive and practical at the same time. Not only did I learn through reading the text book, doing the weekly assignments; but also in the one-on-one coaching that I received from my assigned Christian Life Coach. I was able to participate as a client; which further enhanced my learning experience as I witnessed firsthand professional coaching modeled for me. I have used this valuable training to grow personally in my involvement with Toastmasters International, where I have been able to successfully compete in Area and Regional Speech Competitions and also earn my Distinguished Toastmaster (DTM) Award which is the highest achievement you can earn. I now use the Coaching techniques and strategies that I learned from PCCCA to mentor other fellow Toastmasters to help them grow into more effective communicators and leaders.

~ Brian Richards, California
Certified Christian Life Coach

I am so grateful that I chose the Professional Christian Coaching and Counseling Academy to provide me with a quality life coaching program in which I earned certifications as both a Christian Life Coach and a Professional Life Coach. It is important to me to have training that is rooted in the Christian faith. The program is a great value, too! After earning those certifications, I went on to study for and earn certifications in Joy Restoration, Christian Grief Coaching, and Stress Relief Coaching. I always integrate the principles of those programs into my life coaching practice. I have benefited so much from Dr. Bush's teachings and well-researched and presented curriculum. I took advantage of a rare opportunity to work with Dr. Bush in a live class that provided me the tools to become better at marketing my practice and converting potential clients into clients. I think the biggest benefit I received (and there are **so** many!) is remembering I must live above reproach. Dr. Bush reminds students of this, and this type of living extends into our marketing, personal social media pages, and anywhere else we leave our footprints.

~ Amy Walton, Virginia
Certified Graduate of Multiple PCCCA Courses

Thank you Dr. Bush. Becoming a Grief and Joy Restoration coach has literally change my life. I am in the military and due to retire within a couple of months. Thanks to the training I received through PCCCA I am now a certified as a CJRC/CCGC. Since obtaining my certifications. I have embarked on this journey to be able to change lives and help people to heal from grief. I am also a newly published author. Thanks to PCCCA. I will start my coaching business full time in the spring of 2017. I am super excited. The training I received is the cornerstone for my new business. I could not be happier and more thankful for this opportunity. The training has really changed my life. Thank you Dr Bush. To God be the Glory.

~ Vernessa Blackwell, Maryland
Certified Joy Restoration Coach / Certified Christian Grief Coach, Author

I am building a school to take in students who have failed to continue their education through the state education system because of Dr. Leelo Bush's coaching lessons. Her lessons and books have transformed my life. Thank God for her beautiful, life-changing coaching.
~ *Mervyn Gabarura, Papua New Guinea*

I feel more in control of my mind, my health and my daily routine. The course modules are created with excellence and are very easy to follow.
~ *Margaret Rowlett, Florida*
Certified Joy Restoration Coach / Certified Christian Grief Coach

I would love to take the opportunity to publicly thank Dr. Bush for the coach training material she has provided for me as I embark on my journey towards becoming a Certified Christian Life Coach. The most helpful aspect for me so far has been the way that the course has been written. It is methodical, easy to follow and understand. It has been invaluable for me to have something which is both Biblically sound and gives me a guide on how to keep my work Spirit-led also. These things are all very important to me. There are so many other courses out there these days, but I have not seen anything with such high standards of excellence while being so easy to relate to and on-task as this one. Thank you Dr. Bush and Rev. Evan Bush. May the Lord continue to use you and your training in order to offer excellence and Biblically sound guidance to God's people.
~ *Marlene Bond, Australia*

All praise to our God for the Counseling classes! I have learned so much and my certification has opened new doors for me. I discovered as I was writing assignments that I have been called to a specific ministry to prevent divorces from happening - before the covenant of marriage has been made! The Lord revealed Truth to the first couple I counseled and divorce was prevented as they chose not to go their separate ways based on the Truth revealed. I credit, first, The Lord God Almighty and then PCCCA with the insight I had received through the counseling course. I recommend this course for any self-starter. It is thorough and truly Biblically based.
~ *Audrey Griffith, Pastor's Wife, Texas*
Certified Graduate of Multiple PCCCA Courses

I know God has called me to walk alongside those who have had all types of losses and deal with grief. I have recently started the Joy Restoration coach training. This course has revolutionized my thinking on grief and how our mind and heart is closely connected. The equipping I am getting from this course is bringing a deeper healing to my own heart and soul. I know when I complete this course I will be well equipped to help many people. I will be able to present to them the hope and joy they can have by choosing to renew their minds by changing their thought patterns which will free them from the fear that grips them. I will equip them with the tools needed to expand their comfort zone by doing things in a new way. I would recommend this course to all counselors, mentors and coaches. It will set you apart from the way the world views grief and healing that is needed to take place in our minds and heart.
~ Tina Young, Minnesota
Certified Joy Restoration Coach / Certified Christian Grief Coach

Becoming a Christian Life Coach created a gateway for speaking life to others with the hope of helping them to recognize their potential and discover the calling upon their lives. I have researched many certification programs however I knew in my heart that I could not settle for just any program. I desired a course that believes in true transformation, which can only come from having a relationship with God; and this program is designed on that premise. I would like to thank Dr. Bush for following the leading of the Holy Spirit, and providing the opportunity for me, to discover my God-given purpose, and the courage to walk-out my unique path.
~ Marilyn Owens, Texas
Certified Christian Life Coach

Table of Contents

Acknowledgements   vii
Introduction   ix

ONE
Journey Through The Narrow Gate   1

TWO
Biblical Coaching Foundation   11

THREE
Coaching Basics   21

FOUR
Internal Changes For The Coach   33

FIVE
Avoiding Detours to Your Destiny   39

SIX
Successful Coaches and Training   49

SEVEN
Faith, Scripture and Communication   55

EIGHT
Coachable or Uncoachable?   65

NINE
Ten Christian Coaching Proficiencies   75

TEN Coaching Systems, Methods, or Models	87
ELEVEN Values-Based Life Design	93
TWELVE Purposeful Passion & Finding Yours	101
THIRTEEN Developing Clear Vision & Mission Statements	107
FOURTEEN Dealing with Change	117
FIFTEEN Overcoming Obstacles	127
SIXTEEN Necessary Listening Skills	137
SEVENTEEN Anatomy of Coaching Sessions	151
EIGHTEEN Practical Procedures & Operations	155
NINETEEN Business/Practice Overview	163
TWENTY Marketing & Branding	177
TWENTY ONE Coaching Business Questions & Answers	191
TWENTY TWO The Uncompromised Truth about Niches	199
TWENTY THREE Ethics, Accountability, & Best Practices	209

TWENTY FOUR
Future of Christian Coaching & Professional Growth   217

My Prayer For You   225
Bibliography   227
About The Author   229
Index   235

Acknowledgements

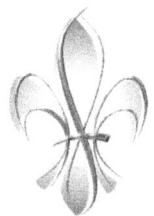

First and foremost, I thank God, for allowing me the privilege to share a very important message. I am grateful to have had the original manuscript of this book edited by Debbie Stankovich, MCLC, FCBA for the first edition in 2009. Her work laid a wonderful foundation for the creation of this second edition. I also want to thank contributors: Kathy Bateman, MCLC, Todd Miller, MCLC, Pastor Florine Milligan, MCLC, Jenny Grace Morris, MCLC and Debbie Stankovich, MCLC, for their contributions to the text. Special thanks go to Shanmugapriya Balasubramanian for expert design and layout of the inside pages of the second edition. I also want to acknowledge the numerous faith leaders and visionaries too many to name, who inspired and encouraged me to write this book. It was time for someone to create and teach authentic, Christian, biblically-based life coaching and yes, even defend our faith in the process. I am humbled and grateful God chose me for this mission. Finally, I thank my husband Evan Bush, MCLC, who has remained supportive, inspirational, and patient throughout the arduous re-writing and editing process. Your love means more to me than you will ever know.

Introduction

Have you heard it said that necessity is the mother of invention? Years ago, I distinctly felt the Holy Spirit impress on me to "stop the compromise". Since then I have developed programs and built a Christian coaching academy where the love of God and truth of His Word are paramount. I initially began writing this book so that the students of the Professional Christian Coaching and Counseling Academy (PCCCA) would have a comprehensive, biblical textbook for Christian coach training, one I had not found elsewhere. Don't get me wrong. There are some wonderful books on the subject, and several are cited here. But I felt a need to supply not only a purely biblical message but also the business and marketing tools that are sorely lacking for many Christian coaches.

In this book you will find scripture upon scripture that demands a pure message. So by the grace of God, I am doing my best to give you just that. Further, learning to coach is only 50% of developing your coaching practice. The other 50% (and sometimes more) is comprised of business and marketing. There is no way around this. I tell prospective students all the time that they might become the world's greatest coach, but if they don't know how to run a business and market their abilities, they won't be able to impact very many lives and they will go broke trying. That is why presenting the entire message of skill and promotion is critical. I truly believe if there is one Christian coaching book you must read, it is this one, because herein lies the truth.

One spring morning in 1997, during the praise and worship portion of our Sunday service, I remember these words coming to me: "I want you to do your own thing." In a heartbeat, I knew the words were given to me by the Holy Spirit. At that moment, I knew I had been called into some type of ministry.

> "When the entire truth is not being taught to prospective Christian coaches and leaders, how can they in turn lead people to the truth of God's Word?"

My first response was to ask, "Why me, Lord?" To this, I remember the reply was: "I need someone in your "flavor". Isn't it interesting how God speaks to us in contemporary words, without saying thee, thou, or other formalities?

When I asked, "Why me?" it wasn't out of reluctance to serve. Rather, I was astounded and humbled that God would think enough of me, to want ME to serve HIM. I was so excited; I wanted to share it with everyone I knew. But as it is with personal revelations, not everyone understood or received this information with the same joy as I did because they knew me before.

Like some of you, I hadn't led a perfect life. I had made my share of mistakes and experienced failures, both personally and in business. Yet I was one of many, perhaps like you, who had been tried and tested by life. I was willing to let God use me for a higher purpose. I was one of the "whosoever will" people that God is looking for.

My prayer is that God uses me and this book to share the truth about the topic of coaching, and Biblical Christian coaching in particular, to move believers from faith to action.

The longer I train Christian coaches, the more I learn about the variety of worldviews among coaching professionals in general and specifically Christian coaches and Christian training programs. Many Christian coaches have shared their concern about the reluctance some churches have shown toward coaching. Based on what I have learned during my time developing the material for this book, I understand the problem and also its solution.

Until 2009, when I wrote the first edition, most Christian coaching had been compromised by being integrated with secular philosophies. Still today, some Christian coaching schools have voluntarily sought secular and new-age accreditation and man's approval. When the entire truth is not being taught to prospective Christian coaches and leaders, how can they in turn lead people to the truth of God's Word? Now, coaching is far more accepted in churches. But sadly, some high-level leadership believed the propaganda that only certain secular organizations are credible to train and certify coaches and consequently only allowed those with compromised training to lead their flocks. Surely this must make the Holy Spirit weep. We must agree in prayer that the truth of God's word prevails.

Church leaders had been afraid of giving up traditional ways of doing things so instead brought in a Trojan horse.

In my first edition, Christian Coaching was refined and can currently be taught from a biblical, Spirit-led worldview exclusively. When we continue to teach it correctly and coach in full agreement with God's Word, eliminating humanistic and new-age devices, affiliations and compromise, then and only then, will it be so greatly anointed by God that no man or leader will be able to contain its power or breadth.

Our charge now is to stop the compromise once and for all. Stop diluting the Word of God, and cease integrating secular philosophies. When we do this, God will bless the Christian coaching movement, and we will see huge numbers across the globe blessed by it. When we are faithful and God sees that our coaching is devoid of apostasies, we can then begin to impact previously unimaginable numbers.

Like many of the authors who came before me, I too have a counseling background. In addition, I am an entrepreneur at heart, a business person, with a lifetime of experience with start-up businesses, advertising, marketing, operating budgets, branding, etc. I have had some phenomenal successes and a few dismal failures as well. But the ones that didn't work out so well were my training ground. God used those experiences to teach and grow me, personally and professionally. I believe God has designed me as a marketplace ministry leader and trainer. I am having the most fun when I am birthing businesses or brainstorming with a client or associate, planning their enterprise and their strategies. All it takes is a starting point to get the ideas flowing.

I have also been blessed with a great faith in God where nothing is impossible. The well-known slogan of the United States Armed Forces: "*The difficult we do immediately; the impossible takes a little longer,*" may as well apply to the way I perceive my world. A very similar quote is actually attributed to a French Minister in 1873, Charles Alexandre de Calonne (1734–1802), who said "*Si c'est possible , c'est fait; impossible? cela se fera.*" In other words "... if a thing is possible, consider it done; the impossible? That *will* be done." (quoted in J. Michelet **Histoire de la Révolution Française** (1847) i . ii. 8).

I truly believe if God calls it into existence, then He will also provide the resources to make it possible. *God knows the plans He has for us, not to hurt us, but to give us hope and a future.* (Jeremiah 29:11) We can proceed confidently as God is with us and He will never leave us or forsake us. He will often take us to uncharted territory though. He wants us to rely on Him. If we already knew how to do everything He asks for, then we would get the idea that we achieved it out of our own ability. Launching out into the unknown requires us to lean on Him. In this way, when we are successful, it is God who gets the glory.

I expect this edition as well, will make some waves. The truth always does. It is my prayer that the knowledge and insight within these pages will persuade each reader to see we should not compromise. I also pray for your strength and the courage of convictions to make the needed changes and fully follow Jesus, embracing the Word, which is fully sufficient to do everything according to God's plan. My prayer is that you are incredibly blessed by what you read here. But I am not writing this book to make friends or please multitudes. God gave me this message and my job is to deliver it so that His Word can set the captives free.

If you already consider yourself a Christian coach but have not been trained biblically, then this book might shake up what you believe to be Christian coaching. Good.

Why good? Because what is contained on these pages, is what God wants *you* to know. Often as I wrote this, I prayed and asked God to use this book to put forth exactly what you, the reader, need. Some of what the Holy Spirit inspired surprised even me. But you see, the duty is mine to deliver the message. The results belong *only* to God. So if you find yourself questioning previously held beliefs or are stunned with the straightforward truth you find between these pages, I strongly recommend you take it up to my boss through prayer. I am confident His words will not return void. At the very least, this book will change your life and how you view Christian coaching.

Herein lies the recipe for genuine, uncompromised, Spirit-led, Christian, biblical coaching along with cutting edge, practical tools for professional, business development, and marketing.

If you are already so excited you can barely sit still to read this book, I have FREE mini-courses for you that will be delivered right to your email box. Get yours now at http://pccca.org/free/.

ONE

Journey Through The Narrow Gate

If God designed you to be a Christian coach, He has a particular, special life in mind for you. Christian coaching can take many forms including professional services, ministry, and personal development. Christian coaches are thought of by some as personal pastors. Others see us as catalysts because we help people make some type of change in their lives, all the while seeking alignment with God's plan for them.

Before we sojourn into the world of Christian coaching, let us take a closer look at what God expects of us personally. "...for unto whomsoever much is given, of him shall be much required..." Luke 12:48 (KJV) When we are given more responsibility as leaders, we are held to a brand new and higher level of accountability.

> "We are all works in progress and have areas that need improvement."

I Timothy 3 outlines the criteria for selecting church leaders. Similarly, any believer in a leadership role, and coaching is a bona fide leadership category, should be of high moral character. Coaches should live their lives above reproach, being trustworthy and self-controlled. We have all heard stories of those who made serious errors in judgment and consequently tarnished the reputation of Christians. God does not need any more people making Him look bad. Please stop here and read I Timothy 3 so you are familiar with this scripture.

If you feel you have not quite arrived at such a place of maturity, you are certainly not alone. We are all works in progress and have areas that need improvement. Now, however, is the time to get your life in order. It all begins by knowing what the Word of God says. We cannot walk in its power or fulfill God's plan if we do not know what is available to us. A great place to begin is with Christian coach training. If you are new to Christian coaching, be aware not all training programs containing the word "Christian" in the title are solely Christian. Though used originally to describe a person who lives according to the teachings of Jesus, the word "Christian" is used very loosely today. These days when you ask someone if they consider themselves Christian, you might get responses like, "I try to live a good life," or "Yes, I believe there is a God."

> "BLESSED (happy, fortunate, prosperous, and enviable) is the man who walks and lives not in the counsel of the ungodly [following their advice, their plans and purposes], nor stands [submissive and inactive] in the path where sinners walk, nor sits down [to relax and rest] where the scornful [and the mockers] gather. But his delight and desire are in the law of the Lord, and on His law (the precepts, the instructions, the teachings of God) he habitually meditates (ponders and studies) by day and

> by night. And he shall be like a tree firmly planted [and tended] by the streams of water, ready to bring forth its fruit in its season; its leaf also shall not fade or wither; and everything he does shall prosper [and come to maturity]." — Psalm 1:1

> "Enter through the narrow gate; for wide is the gate and spacious and broad is the way that leads away to destruction, and many are those who are entering through it. But the gate is narrow (contracted by pressure) and the way is straightened and compressed that leads away to life, and few are those who find it. Beware of false prophets, who come to you dressed as sheep, but inside they are devouring wolves. You will fully recognize them by their fruits...." — Matthew 7:13-16

You will not know the significance of the work God wants to do through you until you are prepared for His call. You need to become excellent as a coach and you need to become excellent personally.

Excellence and Other Qualities of a Christian Life Coach

Excellence Paradigm versus Success Paradigm

A paradigm is a way of thinking or processing information based on foregone conclusions, which influence us so much it affects the overall way we view our life. *The Encarta Dictionary* describes a paradigm as an example that serves as a pattern or model for something, especially one that forms the basis of a methodology or theory (The Encarta Dictionary).

In the world's way of thinking, particularly in secular and new-age coaching, the desired outcome to any goal is SUCCESS! It sounds great to achieve what one sets out to accomplish. Yet an important ingredient is missing from success by itself. A person could steal something and not get caught, thereby successfully stealing it. But as Christians, morally and ethically we should not coach someone to act in a way that goes against biblical teaching. Therefore, for our purposes here, we aim at EXCELLENCE as the *Bible* instructs. We know that when we achieve new levels of EXCELLENCE, success will be a by-product of it. No scripture puts these priorities into perspective better than the following verse:

> "But seek ye first the kingdom of God, and his righteousness; and all these things shall be added unto you." — Matthew 6:33 (KJV)

OUR GOAL ⇨ EXCELLENCE

In his April 1, 1999 article entitled "Excellence Is Better than Success," Moishe Rosen, founder of Jews for Jesus says, "Excellence is better than success. It entails pleasing God—fulfilling one's destiny as His child—godliness. Godliness does not lead us to strive for success, but to strive for excellence—to strive to accomplish God's purposes, thus fulfilling our highest calling as His redeemed ones. How we love to quote Romans 8:28: '...*all things work together for good...*' But we must be careful to remember the rest of the verse: '...*to those who are the called according to His purpose.*'"

When you read the rest of that passage, you find that God calls us to be conformed to the image of His Son. We are not all called to be professional missionaries. We are not all called to be preachers, or for that matter Christian life coaches. But we are all called to fill and fulfill a definite role within the body of Christ. As those who have received the Spirit of Christ, we know what God asks of us. We also know deep inside when we settle for doing or giving Him something less than He asks.

<small>The following article appeared in the Mt. Juliet Messenger on April 25, 1999, and also appears on the church website at http://www.mtjuliet.org/nine_steps_to_achieving_christ/</small>

Nine Steps to Achieving Christian Excellence

"And yet I show you a more excellent way" — *I Corinthians 12:31*

1. DECIDE you want to excel.

"...that you may approve the things that are excellent" — *Philippians 1:10*

2. FOLLOW the apostles' pattern.

"Therefore, brethren, stand fast and hold the traditions which you were taught, whether by word or our epistle." — *II Thessalonians 2:15*

3. CONCENTRATE on what works for you.

"For as the body is one and has many members, but all the members of that one body, being many, are one body, so also is Christ. Now you are the body of Christ, and members individually." — *I Corinthians 12:12, 27*

4. TAKE the INITIATIVE and START

"Whatever your hand finds to do, do it with your might..." — Ecclesiastes 9:10

5. CONCENTRATE on the benefits as well as the obligations.

"His lord said to him, 'Well done, good and faithful servant; you have been faithful over a few things, I will make you ruler over many things. Enter into the joy of your lord.'" — Matthew 25:23

6. REMEMBER the past to help you, but not to hurt you.

"...forgetting those things which are behind and reaching forward to those things which are ahead, I press toward the goal for the prize of the upward call of God in Christ Jesus." — Philippians 3:13-14

7. BE CONFIDENT, but not conceited.

"For God has not given us a spirit of fear, but of power and of love and of a sound mind." — II Timothy 1:7

8. COMPARE with others for motivation, but not to despair.

"Imitate me, just as I also imitate Christ." — I Corinthians 11:1

9. PERSEVERE.

"And we desire that each one of you show the same diligence to the full assurance of hope until the end, that you do not become sluggish, but imitate those who through faith and patience inherit the promises." — Hebrews 6:11-12

Essential Qualities

As Christian life coaches, we must be aware that we are influential and that such influence must be Godly. While we do not tell our clients what to do, we need to frame our questions to them in such a way that our clients see leadership within us. Why do we ask questions, rather than telling our clients what they should do?

First, Jesus modeled this technique for us. He usually asked questions in order to achieve results. Second, if your client comes up with their own answer, they are three times more likely to act on the solution when they "own" it. Third, we recognize "If we give a man a fish, we feed him for a day. But if we teach a man to fish, we feed him for a lifetime." (exact origin unknown)

In his book, *Spiritual Leadership*, J. Oswald Sanders (Sanders, 1994) lists what he calls "Essential Qualities of Leadership." These include:

Discipline
Vision
Wisdom
Decision
Courage
Humility
Integrity and Sincerity

Why do you suppose the author lists "discipline" first? Because, as Sanders puts it, "Without this essential quality, all other gifts remain as dwarfs: they cannot grow. So discipline appears first on our list. Before we can conquer the world, we must first conquer the self."

> "*I* believe that even though not all of us are called to leadership within organizations, every Christian has an influence over those he or she comes in contact with."

At the Professional Christian Coaching and Counseling Academy, we frequently hear questions regarding why our programs are set up in particular modules with precise outlines of what must be accomplished for each. The reason is to develop discipline. Excellence cannot be achieved in any facet of our lives or in the coaching relationship without discipline.

Exercise

On a blank sheet of paper, please list the *Essential Qualities* shown on the previous page. Please write a paragraph about each one, telling why it is important.

Leadership

It is every Christian's duty to be the best he or she can be for God. Like anything we undertake, if our coaching abilities can be improved, we should do and learn all we can so we can become excellent. We have a responsibility to be the best we can be as ambassadors for Christ. One of the worst things we can do is act in such a way as to turn someone away from God.

Continuing Education

> *"Study and be eager and do your utmost to present yourself to God approved (tested by trial), a workman who has no cause to be ashamed, correctly analyzing and accurately dividing (rightly handling and skillfully teaching) the Word of Truth." — II Timothy 2:15*

If you are planning a career in coaching, you might as well reconcile yourself to a life that includes continuing your education. Always have a book in process and another in the wings, so to speak. Plan to attend seminars, meetings, conferences, networking opportunities, tele-classes and any learning event you can find. You will need these opportunities for professional training, marketing, self-improvement, and to learn more in order to help your clients. *A good coach is always at least one step ahead of his or her clients.*

Motives & Motivation

As we continue to grow in our faith, we come to realize that God puts great emphasis on our motives. That is why we talk about the differences between seeking excellence and seeking success.

Seeking excellence is doing what we can by the grace of God to come in line with His will and timing, just because He is God. We are looking to serve Him.

Seeking success means doing what we can to elevate ourselves in some way. In this paradigm we are looking to serve ourselves. When we pray for worldly success we are in essence asking God to serve us.

Young Christians

look for what God can do for or give them.

Mature Christians

look for what they can do or give to serve God.

See the difference? When we mature in Christ, we have a paradigm shift. It becomes less about us and more about Him.

Putting God First

The first commandment tells us not to have any other gods before our God. But what does that really mean? In my interpretation, it means I should place no man or thing ahead of my God.

But we really need to examine what it means to put someone first. It is easier to imagine when we are talking about someone we love. We think about them and talk about them all the time. We crave the time we spend with them and want to spend more and more time in their presence. We hang onto their every word. They are very important to us. We want to do whatever we can to please them and make them happy, because we love them. Tasks that are otherwise tedious become labors of love.

Exercise

Think about your relationship with God. Are you putting God first? Are you spending regular quality time with God and the Word? Think about what it would take for you to put God first and write a 250-300 word essay about what it means to you to put God first in your life and anything you may have to change in order to get your life on the track God wants it to be. Then consider practical steps you can take starting today.

Your Role as a Christian Life Coach

As a Christian life coach, your role is more important than that of any other type of coach. By this I mean not only do you address and partner with your clients to achieve their objectives, but you also need to stand as a barometer, helping your clients see whether they are growing closer to God or farther away.

You may have entered coaching because you want to help others and make them feel good. That is all fine and well. However there may come times when you have to say some tough things—things you would rather not say. Occasionally, and only as the Holy Spirit leads, you may need to lovingly tell your clients that some part of what they are doing is out of alignment with the Word. To do this you will need to know the Word of God. Always pray for discernment and to know what to say. Ask the Holy Spirit to give you the exact words you need at that time. Become a Luke 12:12 Christian life coach.

> "For the Holy Spirit will teach you in that very hour and moment what [you] ought to say." — Luke 12:12

Be a Seeker of Truth

The Bible tells of a time when there will be many deceptions. New-age coaching philosophies, tools, and strategies give clients the impression all answers can be found from within. We maintain the Holy Bible is the final authority. As a Christian life coach and ambassador for Christ, you need to maintain the truth.

> "For the time will come when [people] will not tolerate (endure) sound and wholesome instruction, but, having ears itching [for something pleasing and gratifying], they will gather to themselves one teacher after another to a considerable number, chosen to satisfy their own liking and to foster the errors they hold, and will turn aside from hearing the truth and wander off into myths and man-made fictions. — II Timothy 4:3-4

Become Disciplined

"Operate in self-control and don't allow your spirit to be unruly. Refuse to be like a city that is broken down and without walls. Self-control and discipline add protection to your life." Paraphrased from Proverbs 25:28

"Seriously consider what you are doing before taking on new projects. Expand prudently and do not court neglect of present duties, by assuming too many new ones." Paraphrased from Proverbs 31:16

Walk In Love

"Love is long-enduring and is patient and kind. Love never envies or becomes jealous. Love is not boastful and does not act haughtily. It is not conceited or arrogant. Love is not rude and does not act unbecomingly. Love does not insist on its own way. Love is not touchy or bitter or resentful. Love does not remember evil done to it. Love does not rejoice with injustice but rather rejoices when fairness and truth prevail." From I Corinthians 13

> "Chosen by God for this new life of love, I dress in the wardrobe He picked out for me: compassion, kindness, humility, quiet strength, discipline. I am even-tempered, content... quick to forgive an offense. I forgive as quickly and completely as the Master forgave me. And regardless of what else I put on, I wear love. It is my basic, all-purpose garment. I never want to be without it." — *Colossians 3:12-14 (The Message)*

I believe this first chapter has given you a good foundation for seeking excellence. No matter how well you have mastered these areas, there is always a new level you can achieve. Make studying the Word, walking in love, knowing and speaking the truth, and personal integrity your inseparable companions.

Exercise

On a separate sheet of paper, please write your own specific commitment to excellence and sign it with today's date.

TWO

Biblical Coaching Foundation

My offices receive phone calls daily from prospective Christian coaching students, and they each have their own circumstances, unique sets of values, and beliefs. I recommend that each of them interview trainers and heads of schools if possible. There should be a mission, faith statement, or both on the school's website.

Ask pertinent questions about their faith, and be as direct as you like. Authentic Christian trainers, schools, and coaches will not be offended by your questions. They will be prepared and happy to share their faith perspectives. In the early years, I would field

all inquiry calls. Now my assistant has taken over that task, yet I still perform many of the enrollment interviews. It is critical to make sure the training and the student's goals are a good match.

> "Authentic Christian trainers, schools, and coaches will not be offended by your questions."

There are few things sadder to me than someone with good intentions who thought they were getting authentic, biblical training only to find out later they had been misled. Naturally, that experience left them afraid to trust anyone and who could blame them?

"See to it that no one carries you off as spoil or makes you yourselves captive by his so-called philosophy and intellectualism and vain deceit (idle fancies and plain nonsense), following human tradition (men's ideas of the material rather than the spiritual world), just crude notions following the rudimentary and elemental teachings of the universe and disregarding [the teachings of] Christ (the Messiah)." — Colossians 2:8

The really scary thing is that it is almost impossible to tell authentic biblical training from imposters. Sometimes even the trainers are just not educated in God's Word enough to know right from wrong. Let me give you an example. Almost all Christian coach training at this time will teach you there are two types of vision, discovered vision and created vision, both of which are taught as perfectly valid. This is just not the case. There are indeed two types of vision but the above are not correct. The two in reality are: God-given and man-made. One is perfect, and the other is flawed. Do you know which is which? Below are some coach training philosophies:

Secular and New-Age

These courses and schools generally separate one's faith from the profession of coaching. They encourage the coach to set aside their own beliefs during their work so as not to interfere with what the clients are trying to achieve. The sessions revolve around the clients' goals as derived from their own thoughts, feelings, and values.

They presume going in that the client is capable of changing their destiny simply by changing their thoughts and actions. These philosophies are considered humanistic.

Christian Varieties

Christian Track – Definition: courses that have Bible verses added into the program to make the casual and not-so-well educated believer comfortable. These programs may be offered by a secular school or organization so they can claim to offer a "Christian" course or track of study. These programs are roughly based on secular course features instead of new-age philosophies. They offer scriptural support for their secular methods. Some programs take scripture out of context to support an unscriptural concept or philosophy.

Apostate – Definition: Apostate training and coaches are counterfeit but look almost identical to the real deal. They may also include neuro linguistic programming (NLP), aura reading, hypnosis, and/or other radically new-age concepts or human manipulation, all of which are completely incompatible with the Word of God. Some trainers and coaches combine rather wacky practices and call them Christian. Learn more about what constitutes apostate by researching "apostate" or "apostasy". Remember that use of the title "Christian" does not necessarily make it so. Satan and his demons are hard at work to deceive, discourage, delay, and defeat the powerful and authentic biblical, Christian coaching movement.

Compromised Programs – Definition: courses that started out Christian or biblical, whose writers or school heads opted for secular or new-age accreditation for falsely perceived gain, thereby coming under the authority of ungodly advisors, consequently compromising course content little by little.

Authentic, Christian Life Coach Training – Definition: Christ-centered, Bible-based, and Spirit-led. These schools staunchly refuse new-age or secular affiliations or accreditation, not wanting to come under the authority of those who might offer unbiblical influence and do not share their faith-based values.

Affiliations and Accreditation

If a coaching school or trainer is accredited by any number of self-appointed, new-age or secular organizations, then regardless of what their program or course is titled, you can count on it meeting the standards of their governing body. Why would they credential anyone who did not share their views?

> *"What is most important to a prospective coaching client is 'Can this coach help me?'"*

In an article written by Emory Hilton-Goode, entitled *The Truth about Coaching School Accreditation*, Hilton-Goode states, "Because there are no universal standards for the life-coaching profession, there are no universal standards for schools. Also, because well-paid coaches generally work in a niche, those niches are such that they are developed by the coach independently of any training they might receive."

What makes the issue of accreditation particularly confusing is marketing. Accreditation is being used as a marketing tool in most cases, not as a barometer of their quality. Many coaching schools are accredited only because a group of colleagues got together and decided to form a group and accredit their associates' schools. How do you know whether this is the case for a school in which you are interested? You really do not know and generally cannot find out.

Many schools use accreditation as a marketing ploy to draw you in and charge exorbitant rates. If you just want to spend more money, go ahead. Price really has little to do with the effectiveness of the materials. The courses offered at the Professional Christian Coaching & Counseling Academy offer the highest level of agreement with God's Word while being highly practical and effective in today's world. Current courses and course-bundles (offering savings) are listed at: http://pccca.org/courses/.

How important is a school's accreditation? Let us put it into realistic perspective. What is most important to a prospective coaching client is "Can this coach help me?" Most clients look to see whether a coach has had formal coach training, but not into the background of the school. And the truth is that clients do not care whether the school you attended is accredited. It just does not come up. Clients will decide to use your services once they are aware of you, if they like you, trust you, feel a connection, and desire the benefits working with you offers. That is pretty much it.

Rey Carr, president of Peer Resources, a recognized world leader in coach training resources, stated "accreditation" in the coaching field has a number of troubling aspects, including its lack of widespread acceptance, conflicts of interests between reviewers and some rated schools, minimal reporting of results, and questionable or vague criteria. While accreditation typically means the school has been reviewed by an external source, it does not necessarily mean that "non-accredited schools" provide less value or poorer quality programs." (Resources)

How will you decide?

You are the one who will ultimately have to make your own choice in this regard. If you want authentic, purely Christian training, the programs exist for you. I know this because I have created the course curriculum for the Professional Christian Coaching and Counseling Academy (http://pccca.org).

But if someone is willing to dilute the truth of God's Word with other world views, there are choices as well. I am not just speaking theoretically. I have real life experience with trying to combine Godly and ungodly. I am not proud of this and I certainly do not believe that way now. Fifteen to twenty years ago, it made perfect, *rational* sense to me that it would only improve a product to combine the God-inspired with the man-made. Now thankfully, I know better.

I suppose integrating philosophies can work in some scenarios, but not if your industry is coaching, where godless and godly worldviews collide. Naturally, everyone believes they are correct. Further, thousands of secular humanists and deceived believers claim that one can only be successful if they are secularly certified and accredited. This propaganda has misled many, well-intentioned believers and convinced them they can have it all if they will only compromise their faith *just a little* with their training and public affiliations. God's Word has a crystal clear message for us in this area:

> "But refuse and avoid irreverent legends (profane and impure and godless fictions, mere grandmothers' tales) and silly myths, and express your disapproval of them. Train yourself toward godliness (piety), [keeping yourself spiritually fit]." — I Timothy 4:7

Why did Jesus come to earth?

This was the first question posed to us in *The Truth Project* (Focus on the Family) session at church. Many answers were offered. Among them were:

- "To save the world."
- "To heal the broken-hearted."
- "God became man, so the world could better understand Him."
- "To offer salvation to the lost."

All of the answers were correct but fell short of the actual reason stated by Jesus himself.

> "God's Word is the only foundation for Christian coaching that contains power to change lives."

"... *This is why I was born, and for this I have come into the world, to bear witness to the Truth ...*" — John 18:37

What is the truth? The truth is God's inerrant plan for mankind. It is laid out in the Holy Bible. As Christians, it is this perspective from which we must coach. And, we cannot coach with the power of this knowledge if we do not know the Word of God. The world is full of those who are not interested in the truth. It was prophesied:

> "For the time is coming when [people] will not tolerate (endure) sound and wholesome instruction, but, having ears itching [for something pleasing and gratifying], they will gather to themselves one teacher after another to a considerable number, chosen to satisfy their own liking and to foster the errors they hold, and will turn aside from hearing the truth and wander off into myths and man-made fictions." — II Timothy 4:3-4

We must keep Christian coaching scripturally sound and pure. God does not need us to fix what He has done, supervise Him, or improve upon what He has already laid out. We must speak out to stop any sort of compromise. *God's Word is the only foundation for Christian coaching that contains power to change lives.*

> "I know that whatever God does, it endures forever; nothing can be added to it nor anything taken from it. And God does it so that men will [reverently] fear Him [revere and worship Him, knowing that He is]" — Ecclesiastes 3:14

When I first entered coaching, I was like many others; eager to learn and join all the industry groups. Yes, this included the secular ones as well. But unbeknownst to me, God had plans for me to become a leader in the Christian coaching movement. I had posted logos and links on my early websites to some of these organizations in order to validate my training, memberships, and position. At that time, I was seeking man's approval, not God's. And God let me know that what I was doing did not please him one bit. I began receiving phone calls from prospective students, one after another, who questioned my faith when they saw what was on my site. One by one, then finally all of the links and logos were removed. The last thing I wanted to do as a believer was give anyone reason to doubt my faith or their own.

Here's a story to bring this home:

A man is trying to teach his children the value of watching wholesome television. "But gee whiz, dad," says his son. "There is just a little bit of violence and profanity in the show. Mostly it's really good!" the young man says enthusiastically.

Understanding his son would need a profound lesson, dad got an idea. Living on a dairy farm, the father went outside and scooped up a spoonful of cow dung. He took it inside and added it into the batter of a cake he was baking.

Later he offered his son a slice of cake, adding "Don't worry son, it only has a little cow dung in it." The boy was immediately repulsed by the idea, and refused to eat the cake.

The father then asked "Are you telling me son that even a little bit of something awful will ruin the whole thing? If you won't eat the cake, why should you watch the show?"

Likewise, I believe even a little bit of ungodly deception can ruin an entire coach training program. Why would a Christian even consider it? After all, it is God who sends the clients. Do you think He will send you more clients if you are not completely committed to Him during your training? We know it is God who promotes us and He does so when we prove ourselves to be ready.

We need look no further than the Parable of Talents to see that God similarly, gives us an opportunity to show Him our heart.

> *"His master said to him, 'Well done, good and faithful servant. You have been faithful over a little; I will set you over much. Enter into the joy of your master."* — Matthew 25:23

Want God to promote you? Study and prepare yourself. Practice and hone your skills to demonstrate that you are ready to serve Him.

A Heart Issue:

Do you desire to wholly serve God? Then you must learn to coach from a purely Christian world view. Those who plan to integrate other sorts of messages and tools into Christian coaching, may unknowingly be saying they know better than God.

If we set anything or anyone (including ourselves) before all of who God is, then we become guilty of idolatry. This is between us and the Lord. It is a heart issue and though we might fool man, we can't hide from God. He can see what our motivations are, whether we trust Him and what is most important to us. Pray for wisdom, revelation and strength to put God first so that you can be a God-honoring, Christian life coach. When we arrive at this place, God will be able to use us in ways we can't yet imagine. When He sees our heart belongs first to Him, he will bless everything we do.

Are you feeling more cautious now? You are wise to look deeper. Pray about your decisions to ensure a clear leading from the Holy Spirit to proceed. God's Word will not return void.

> *"If any of you lacks wisdom, you should ask God, who gives generously to all without finding fault, and it will be given to you." — James 1:5*

THREE

Coaching Basics

Life coaching in general and Christian life coaching specifically are not counseling or therapy. While they both involve confidential, one-on-one relationships, there are many differences.

Life Coaching

- Is action oriented
- Deals with the present and future
- Helps the client move forward from an already mentally-healthy position
- Helps the client do more, faster than he or she would be able to do on their own
- Helps the client take their goals and themselves more seriously

- Supports the client with exhortation, encouragement and is their #1 cheerleader
- Helps the client strategize and offers suggestions as appropriate

Counseling/Therapy

- Deals with the past
- Works to heal hurts and emotional issues
- Helps the client become healthy and mentally stable
- Is not action oriented as much as discussion on internal issues
- Works with client to help them arrive at their own solutions

More Differences between Coaching and Counseling/Therapy

Coaching and counseling outcomes are generally quite different also. Coaching involves beginning where someone is today and helping them move forward to the best of their ability, to reach their goals and God-given destiny. Someone needs to be functioning reasonably well in their current life for coaching to be effective. Counseling and therapy are focused on healing someone from the past hurts or mental/emotional illness(es).

WHAT IS CHRISTIAN LIFE COACHING?

Should any life coaching performed by a Christian be considered Christian life coaching? Should it be a requirement that both the coach and the person being coached or client be Christians in order for Christian life coaching to take place? Or perhaps, could any person who uses the scriptures from the Holy Bible to support a coaching relationship be considered a Christian life coach? The answers to these questions have varied over the years, depending on the world view of the person answering them.

For the purposes of this book, I think we need to be very clear about the operational definition of a Christian life coach. In order to do this, we need to take a look at what life coaching is.

> *Life coaching involves a collaborative, one-to-one, confidential, ongoing, usually deliberately-formed relationship in which*

the client is guided by the coach to make better decisions, look at alternatives to current choices, identify tolerations, barriers, challenges, reach beyond their feelings of limitations, and focus better to achieve their goals.

Coaching is client-centered and driven, and coach-supported.

Secular coaching urges the coaching client to seek their own desires and goals. It encourages the client to look within themselves for what they really want. The secular coach then works with the client to achieve the client's stated goals and remove obstacles (human, material, and environmental) that get in the way of achieving success. The coach's own values, morals, and feelings may have little or no bearing on the results they help their client attain. The coach remains open and non-judgmental. The sessions are ALL about the client and client's wants, needs, hopes, dreams, desires, and how to achieve them.

Christian coaching inspires the client to seek the Lord's will in their life and align their life with God's plan. This requires the Christian coach to be familiar with biblical principles and especially New Testament teachings of Christ. The Christian coach uses coaching knowledge, proficiencies, and tools to assist the client in finding their talents and gifts to benefit a greater purpose and uses prayer in addition to traditional coaching tools to assist in removal of obstacles presented by the enemy (Satan). In every way, including their own life, the Christian life coach should demonstrate and urge compliance with Godly lifestyles.

> *"**We** are only as limited as God wants us to be."*

Therefore we can say that Christian life coaching is Christ-centered, because relationship with Christ is promoted as the primary foundation for achieving excellence and abundance in one's life. In Matthew 6:33, Jesus tells us to *"... seek first His kingdom and righteousness; and all these things shall be added to you."*

Another difference is that while secular coaching works under man's power and uses man's limited resources, Christian coaching confesses and works in harmony with God's infinite power, aligns with the leading of the Holy Spirit, and avails itself to God's limitless resources and power.

Christian life coaching recognizes that prayer moves the hands of God and God can change the heart and mind of man. Christian coaching recognizes God frequently does not call the equipped, meaning those who know exactly what they are doing. Rather God equips those He calls. It is not up to you and me to come up with all our own solutions nor are we responsible for outcome or results. This relieves the stress from the coach and client related to having to come up with all the solutions and answers from within the client, as secular coaching teaches.

Christian life coaching seeks to find God's leading in which goals to accomplish and also how to go about accomplishing the goals. It seeks the Lord's will and timing in everything.

Another way to approach this is to show the difference between secular and Christian coaching with diagrams. The illustrations shown indicate who is involved in each type of coaching relationship. The black, intersecting areas show where the results emanate from. You will note the second diagram with the three circles has a much larger results area.

Figure I
SECULAR COACHING: The **shaded** area designates the coach-client relationship from where results originate.

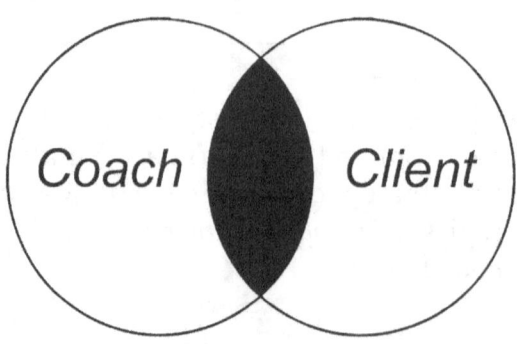

Figure II
SPIRIT-LED CHRISTIAN LIFE COACHING: The **shaded** area designates where the Holy Spirit is involved in the Christian coaching relationship and from where results originate.

Is there anything secular coaches can do that Christian life coaches cannot? Since we are working within the design framework laid out by God himself, in the words found in scripture as well as with the Holy Spirit, we are only as limited as God wants us to be.

Christian life coaching according to our definition, honors the Trinity; God the Father, Jesus Christ the Son, and the Holy Ghost or Holy Spirit. When Jesus returned to the Father, He left so the helper could come to be with us. The "helper" referred to in the Bible is the Holy Spirit.

Do You Have A Calling?

While a great many express an interest in coaching, the most important consideration is to discover whether it is part of God's plan for you to become a life coach. Perhaps you are called to become a professional Christian life coach with a full-fledged coaching practice or business. Maybe you are meant to use coaching skills within your current or other, new profession. It could be that God wants you to use coaching skills within your church or ministry. Perhaps you do not possess any particular passion for organized coaching, but you discover that you can encourage and enrich the lives of those with whom you come into contact. All of these scenarios are perfectly valid reasons for you to become educated about Christian coaching.

There are many signs to look for in determining whether God has ordained you to be coaching. Which of the following apply to you?

- You have been approached by friends, family and/or associates for your opinion.
- Others respect your opinion and frequently take advice from you.
- You have the gift of exhortation. By this I mean it comes naturally to you to lift others up and encourage them in life's journeys.
- One of your greatest joys in life is to see others around you happy, fulfilled, and achieving success.
- You are relatively well organized in your personal life.
- You have many life experiences and are willing to share your own testimony in order to help others.
- You have accepted the Lord, Jesus Christ as your Savior.

There are more, but the above are just a few indicators, in no particular order of importance, that God may be calling you to coaching.

Reasons People Want Christian Life Coaching

The reasons are probably as many as there are people seeking Christian life coaching. However, there are general subjects that come up again and again. Some of these are:

- To find one's life purpose
- To get values clarification
- Time management
- Stress reduction
- To develop a better, closer relationship with God
- To get help dealing with change
- To overcome obstacles
- To develop better professional skills

- To change careers or seek promotion
- To move forward faster because of accountability to the coach

And more.

Teach a Man to Fish

Recently I received a career evaluation from a young man on the West Coast. He was just starting out in his counseling career and wanted to add coaching to his marketable skills. At the point where the form asked about his criteria for the course he hoped to select, he stated in bold letters: "one that will teach me everything about client retention."

I could see from this response that he was from the school that in order to have a full practice, he needed to retain as many as possible of his current clients. This view was not about his clients' well-being and progress. It was all about his own income and likely he lacked faith in God to provide for him.

My opinion about client retention is very close to the one expressed by Gary R. Collins, Ph.D. in his book *Christian Coaching*, where he states, *"As a coach, the goal is to work yourself out of a job so that the person being coached is able to make changes and then move forward without continued assistance."* (Gary R. Collins, 2001)

The philosophy is similar to our Christian fishing analogy. "Give a man a fish and you will feed him for a day. Teach him to fish and you will feed him for a lifetime." I believe as Christian coaches, we must teach people to fish.

The Business Side

You need to realize that having a Christian Coaching Practice is 50% coaching skills and knowledge and 50% business and marketing acumen. You need to ask yourself whether you are excited about the prospect of owning and running your own business. If not, perhaps working for an existing coaching practice or other service organization may be more appealing. You need to assess whether you are so convinced about having a Christian life coaching practice, that you are willing to market your business. Be forewarned, you will not be allowed to hide your light under a bushel! The best that Christ offers us all will only be made manifest when you are able to let others know you are there and ready to help them.

> "Whatever your hand finds to do, do it with all your might..." — Ecclesiastes 9:10

There are many resources to help you run your business and help you learn the marketing involved with becoming successful. You will find marketing information in the business development portion of this book. Your training will lead you in the specific steps you need to take to begin your practice, so there is no need for concern. For advanced marketing and business building, I created the Spirit Led Marketing© course found at http://pccca.org/slm/.

But you should consider whether you can see yourself being a Christian life coach and sharing that with others. If you can, then you have a world full of opportunities. If not, you may become a great coach who rarely gets to work with any clients. By all means, do not wait to coach others until you think you know everything.

As I was doing my devotions one morning not long ago, I found the most awesome scripture to support you in your training. As I coach and train others who coach, I often hear that a person did not start a project or take a particular action because they did not feel "ready" to do so. I know of many times personally when in the past, I did not take an action and then blamed it on not feeling ready.

Do you realize the larger our dreams and visions, the less likely we would ever be to step out if we wait to feel ready?

I learned from my reading in Ephesians 3 that even though we may not know how to do something, we **do** know God, the one who knows everything! We know that God has limitless resources. Ephesians 3:20 tells us that He is able to do exceedingly, abundantly over and above anything we could dare to hope, ask, or think. If God wants you to do something, He will give you the inner and outer means to do it.

It is very natural for us to delay until we feel that we are really ready, but God usually does not ask us to do only those things we are prepared to do. If He did, He would not get the glory.

We can remain confident God knows what He is doing. This allows us to be ready to move forward as we are led by the Holy Spirit. Interestingly, when we wait to feel ready before we move forward, we are actually leaning on our own resources instead of God. Those who have visited my office know I have a plaque over my desk that says, "Duty is mine, the results are God's." When we get into the results area, we are trying to do God's job so no wonder we lose our peace.

> "**D**uty is mine, the results are God's"

"So many people say 'I'm just not ready.' The business isn't perfect. I don't have enough experience, credentials, resources or (_____) fill in the blank. I want to encourage you, 'ready' is a myth," says Christy Wright, business coach on Dave Ramsey's team.

"Ready is not real," Christy continues. "You will never wake up and feel totally ready to do the thing you want to do that you are scared to do. So you just do it anyway. Start now, start tomorrow. You put yourself out there. It's by doing that you learn and it's by doing that you gain that experience. It's by doing that you get the confidence to take the very next step. I want to encourage you. **Ready is a myth**. You can start tomorrow. Give yourself permission to be a beginner and start somewhere."

My husband, Evan Bush, who is a Certified Master Christian Life Coach and president of the Professional Christian Coaching and Counseling Academy, likes to put it this way, "In order for God to direct your path, you need to step out. The waters of the Red Sea did not part until someone stepped out. Even if you step out in the wrong direction, God can guide and re-direct you from there. But God can't and won't guide a stationary object."

Your first step is a step of faith. God will do for us as much as we are willing to believe Him for. So if you have been waiting for a sign from God to move forward to your destiny, ***this*** is that sign. Do not wait until you are completely ready. Make sure God gets the glory!

TYPES OF CHRISTIAN COACHES

The Coaching Practitioner/Purist

This type of coach will hold firm to asking questions in order to facilitate the client's progress towards a goal. Their variety of coaching is supportive, maintains accountability and is largely geared to engender execution of agreed-upon actions.

This coach feels the optimum coaching experience is gained by working one-on-one with the client and thus, only offers personal coaching. This coach also struggles with describing what coaching is to their client. They feel they must demonstrate coaching in order to maintain credibility.

These coaches seem to struggle with income. It is difficult to justify why someone would pay for this type of coaching since the coach does not claim to offer specific solutions and expertise.

The Coaching Entrepreneur (Marketplace Coach)

The coaching entrepreneur is a strategist and idea person who will confidently share their knowledge and solutions. This coach leads with the solutions they can provide, rather than their tool, which happens to be coaching. This type of coach thinks of themselves as a business person first, coach second. They offer specific solutions and they sometimes don't even mention coaching because it is their communication tool. They promote their solution rather than their tool. The solution connects immediately with their ideal client.

They earn the highest income among coaches, one that is derived from multiple sources that may include product sales, groups, events, speaking engagements and occasionally one-to-one sessions. This coach knows that their time is extremely valuable so one-on-one coaching is reserved as a high-end offer to a select, few clients.

Think of it this way. A car mechanic gets business by telling about his solution, that he repairs cars, rather than his tool, a great, new wrench. How much would he earn if he only talked about the wrench?

Is it really okay to earn a living from Christian coaching?

Moreover, if God wants us to remain humble, is it godly to coach fellow believers to achieve success? The answer to this lies in our motivation.

- Are we coaching because it's our latest idea of how to make money?
- Do we care about genuinely improving the lives of our clients or is it more about bragging rights to certification in the coaching profession?
- Are we using the "Christian" title, so that we can entice believers to follow our own (hidden) agenda?
- Are we using the "Christian" title as a way to legitimize making money from believers?
- Do we call ourselves "Christian coaches" because we go to church, so any type of coaching we do, regardless of where or how trained, would fall under the category of Christian coaching?
- Is it a profession we chose or one that God chose for us? God looks at our heart and knows our motivation.

God knows whether we are just in it for the income or whether our hearts are seeking direction from the Holy Spirit to equip others. If we are involved in works of the flesh or using man-made devices to coach others, our efforts will be largely frustrated. The Bible promises this. The Word says it is God who frustrates our purposes. In I Peter 5:5 it says, "...*For God sets Himself against the proud (the insolent, the overbearing, the disdainful, the presumptuous, the boastful)--[and He opposes, frustrates, and defeats them], but gives grace (favor, blessing) to the humble.*"

Ok, you might think, "this scripture is not talking about me". But wait a minute. Have you ever thought you can do something yourself? Thinking you can do it yourself without God's involvement or input is pride. Many are surprised to discover that it is God himself who will defeat you. Why is it that some Christian coaches struggle and eventually quit? They end in despair because they try to coach or build a business without including God.

And what about all of those who consider themselves Christian and do all sorts of work with wrong motives that leads others away from God, while enjoying reasonable success in the process? I would not want to be them when God calls me home.

> *"Not everyone who says to Me, Lord, Lord, will enter the kingdom of heaven, but he who does the will of My Father Who is in heaven. Many will say to Me on that day, Lord, Lord, have we not prophesied in Your name and driven out demons in Your name and done many mighty works in Your name? And then I will say to them openly (publicly), I never knew you; depart from Me, you who act wickedly [disregarding My commands]."* — Matthew 7:21-23

If you suspect it's time to correct course, do it now.

FOUR

Internal Changes For The Coach

What does it take to have profoundly life-changing coaching sessions? How do we really make an impact on the lives of others? This answer, when I discovered it, was so simple it left me speechless.

The most important thing we have to do is JUST SHOW UP. That may sound too simple, but it's the truth. Unless we show up, not much else can happen. Are we in agreement with that?

Next, I believe we need to pray for, and what is more, *walk in* knowing the Holy Spirit is within us and works through us.

We need to be seeking first the Kingdom and His righteousness. Our duty is to be familiar with God's Word.

*"**B**egin by showing up!"*

Then when we show up, if we happen to run out of resources, the Holy Spirit will work through us and we will speak His message. This removes all fear or nervousness from our sessions because the results are not up to us. All we have to do is show up and leave the results up to God — where they rightfully belong.

But let us keep this in the proper context here. Before we hang out our "Christian Life Coach" shingle, we need to be well-trained so we have the skills our clients need and expect. We owe it to our clients and to God, to be the best we can be. As ambassadors of the Lord, we need to have a hallmark of uncompromising EXCELLENCE.

Some time ago, when I discussed this with my husband and told of events when the Spirit worked or spoke through me, he was at first a little skeptical. He had been raised in a Christian home, but had never experienced miracles or anything he would attribute to the Holy Spirit. Years later when he became a Christian Life Coach and began working with me full time, he found the same thing happening to him as had happened to me. He would come out of coaching sessions with testimonies of his own.

When my students ask me what is the most important thing they need to do as a Christian life coach, I tell them, "BEGIN BY SHOWING UP". Second, pray asking God to guide you.

Our Bodies Are Temples

When we coach others, it is rare to deal exclusively with only one facet of someone's life. Generally, we coach the entire person. We know our work life affects our personal life and our personal life can affect how we perform in our career. Our physical, mental, and spiritual health has to be in good order if we are going to be used by God to help others.

As a reminder to any who need it, the Bible tells us our bodies are the temple of the Holy Spirit. We need to take good care of ourselves, our minds, and our souls. We must be careful about what we allow inside us — including music, television, movies, books and friends.

In Matthew 6:22-23 Jesus tells us that the lamp of our body is our eye. If our eye is good, our whole body will be full of light. But if our eye is bad, our entire body will be full of darkness. Be careful what you watch on television, see at the theatre or allow inside of yourself in any form.

In addition, we should take good care of our physical selves. There are three major reasons.

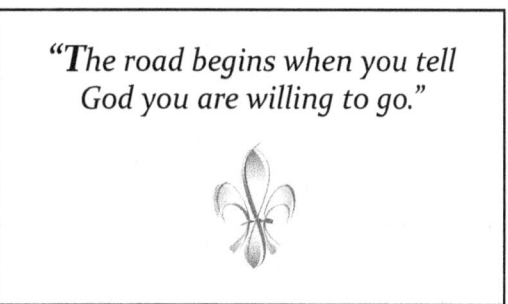

"The road begins when you tell God you are willing to go."

- If we do not feel good, then it will be difficult for us to perform our work with excellence.
- If we do not take care of ourselves and maintain our grooming and appearance, how will we gain the respect of others who would follow our lead? We are the Lord's ambassadors.
- If you had a choice to do business with someone, would you choose a well-groomed, neat individual or a sloppy, unkempt person?

Be mindful of what you eat. Make sure you consume a balanced diet. It may be difficult in our fast-paced world, but plan ahead to eat healthy meals. I made a decision a few years ago, to take better care of myself and lost 30 pounds. My goal was to get healthy, rather than lose weight. Now I want to continue to take excellent care of the body God entrusted to me. I know when I am disciplined in this area, it will help in other areas of my life as well. I also acknowledge if I want God to promote me to the next level, I need to be ready inside and out.

American society sadly, encourages over-eating (gluttony). Compare the size of portions we serve here in the United States to meals in other countries. The Word of God tells us gluttony is a sin and not an insignificant one. Gluttony means "habitual eating to excess" (as defined in www.thefreedictionary.com). It also conveys an obsession with food. Some theologians say that food is symbolic for anything we do in excess. I won't address it much further here, but we do know the Bible discourages excess and promotes moderation and balance. Any obsession is idolatry. We need to be aware of this in our own life and when we coach others.

Who Will Go?

So do you still want to be a Christian life coach? Get ready for the journey of your life.

The road begins when you tell God you are willing to go. Ask Him to use you in whatever humble way He pleases. The Bible tells us the harvest is ready but the laborers are few. If you feel led to become a Christian life coach, then do not delay. Begin by learning all you can about this profession and get linked up with a good training program to become all God wants you to be and receive all He has for you. See course listings at: http://pccca.org/courses/.

Walk in Love

The type of love we need to possess and express is described in I Corinthians 13. This is frequently referred to as the "love chapter" in the Bible. Love is not just a mushy, gushy, romantic feeling we have, which is eros love. It is so much more. Agape love is modeled for us by Jesus. It is a spiritual and selfless model of love. Paraphrased from I Corinthians, when we are walking in agape love...

- we are patient with others.
- we show kindness to them.
- we believe the best in them.
- we do not keep a record of when we have been wronged by others.
- we are slow to anger.
- we don't boast or brag.
- we are not jealous.

- we do not act with haughtiness or arrogant superiority.
- we do not enjoy wrong-doing, but we celebrate righteousness.
- we are not rude or selfish.

Agape love protects, trusts, and hopes. It never gives up. It is not easy nor does it come naturally for most of us to love this way. It takes time and discipline to be mindful of the way we behave toward others. It takes action or lack of action in some cases. It requires careful and mindful response, not hasty action. Yet as ambassadors for Christ and leaders, Christian life coaches need to walk in agape love.

It will serve you well to dedicate some time to study what else the Word of God says about love. Just look up "love" references in any Bible concordance. Then study also the context in which God's Word talks about love. It will be life-changing.

FIVE

Avoiding Detours to Your Destiny

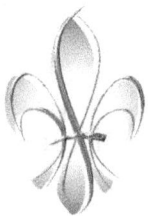

If you have been called by God to coach others, this section will hopefully help you avoid delays and detours to what God is calling you to do. I believe sometimes God is telling us to wait, but other times He is waiting on us to get our lives in order.

Why should Christians practice *only* Christian or Biblical life coaching? I am asked this question weekly, if not daily by coach training applicants, so it seemed appropriate I write on the topic. Just so we are clear about the frame of reference in this section, we presume there are two basic life coaching philosophies or worldviews. One is that all answers we need reside in and come from within a person. That is the new-age (some call it secular) philosophy. The other foundational philosophy is that all answers come from God, His Word in the Holy Bible and/or the leading of the Holy Spirit.

> *"God does not need any more half-truth Christians making fools of themselves in His name."*

Before I delve deeper into this subject, I want to share why I am so passionate about this. For a long time, I have had this passion and it was not until I began composing this book that the Holy Spirit revealed to me the reason why. You see, I am not only sharing a random way of believing with you. I have personally walked this out. Many years ago, I was of the belief that if I glean the "best" of what God has to offer and blend it with the "best" of what man has to offer, I will have the answers to *everything*. As a young believer, it made a lot of sense to me. That is, until I could make no progress. I felt held back at every turn. I was frustrated, even though I thought I had all the answers.

So I was stuck for many years. Looking back, I can see God was not going to raise me up as His representative, until I understood the truth. God, you see, does not need any more half-truth Christians making fools of themselves in His name. God knew the plans He had for me (Jeremiah 29:11), but I had to pass some tests before He would set my work as an example for others. And friends, I did not have anyone to teach me this so I had to work it out for myself. It took me many, frustrating years of being broke and broken before God. I pray you can avoid these detours to your destiny by understanding and believing what I will teach you here.

Why is this foundation important?

Secular coaching, since it is not totally devoid of belief, is actually new-age coaching. *The Merriam Webster Dictionary* defines secular as "of or relating to the worldly or temporal." The word "secular" might also be an abbreviated way of stating secular humanism, which Merriam Webster defines as "humanistic philosophy viewed as a non-theistic religion antagonistic to traditional religion." You see, it is not that secularists have no belief. Their belief is that they want to overlook or disregard any godliness at all. "Non-theistic" was not listed in Merriam Webster, so I looked up the definition of "theistic." "Theistic" means believing in a god or gods. So "non-theistic" would be the opposite or not believing in a god. Somewhere in between are the agnostics. Agnostic is defined as "one who is not committed to believing in either the existence or the nonexistence of God or a god."

For a long time the term "new-age" has been confusing to many, so for more information you may be interested to read details at their website. At https://en.wikipedia.org/wiki/New_Age there is a full description with the origin of "new-age" beliefs. In summary, new-age followers (also known as Universalists) are encouraged to acquire whatever beliefs and practices feel the best and most natural to them. New-age presumes the individual is the best judge of what is correct. Since all beliefs are considered of equal value, none are superior or inferior.

Some of the beliefs held by new-age believers may include pantheism (God is in everything), reincarnation, karma, aura reading, new-world order, guided imagery, hypnosis, need to replace patriotism for global concern, and others. Moreover, all roads lead to God, who is in everyone and everything. Just pick what appeals most to you. There is no right or wrong answer.

Can you see the deception? If there is no right and wrong, all solutions are relative. The increase in new-age believers has incrementally increased the belief in moral relativism. Moral relativists believe no universal standard exists by which one can determine the truth or validity of an ethical proposition. If this is the case, then the strongest among us will make rules at their own whim and enforce the rules justly or unjustly, upon those who are weaker.

Is that the kind of world you want to live in? Most people would answer "no" to that question. Then why won't they believe in God and follow Jesus? For most of them sadly, that would require an accountability for their lifestyle choices that they are unwilling to submit to.

Exercise

Now is the time to consider your own beliefs. Get some paper and write down what you believe in as much detail as possible.

Are you an authentic Christian (Jesus follower, Holy Bible believer)?

If you are, then you acknowledge that universal religion is contrary to biblical teaching. In the Gospel, Jesus teaches us that **only** He is the way, the truth and the life (John 14:6). No one can be saved without Jesus interceding for them. All things are not equal. All paths do not lead to heaven. The road is narrow. People cannot buy their way into heaven just by being good or giving large offerings at church. We are saved by grace through faith when we ask Jesus to be our Savior. Period.

This may be a new concept to some but all men and women are equal before God. What is available to one is available to everyone. All that is required is that one makes the choice to ask for and **receive** their salvation.

> "There is neither Jew nor Greek, there is neither bond nor free, there is neither male nor female: for ye are all one in Christ Jesus." — Galatians 3:28 (KJV)

How does Christian coach training fit into our belief system?

My view and that of the trainers at the Professional Christian Coaching and Counseling Academy (PCCCA) is that all answers come from God, His Word and the Holy Spirit.

Acknowledging that some have not been taught how to discern the leading of the Holy Spirit, here is one criterion to keep in mind. The Holy Spirit will never lead someone to do something not supported by scripture. If what you are considering doing or saying does not agree with the Word of God in the Bible, you can be sure it is not the Holy Spirit's leading.

There are several reasons why Christians (followers of and believers in Jesus Christ) should practice exclusively Christian (meaning scripturally correct and Holy Spirit-led life coaching).

First, we have to ask ourselves: Is there anything man can do or give us that is of greater value or will outperform what God can do or give us?

If you answered a resounding "no" then the answer is clear. There is no reason to study new-age life coaching because it is ineffective and foundationally inaccurate. Certainly there can be some benefit from that form of coaching, but not nearly as much as when God is involved in the process. If coaching is about reaching the highest level possible, then why would we deliberately seek out something less?

I do not want second rate solutions and I will not settle for being second best, so why would I want to clutter my mind or coach others with inferior solutions. Coaching results pre-suppose only the BEST of all possible answers should be selected.

Why not study both Christian and new-age/secular coaching?

Good question. In fact, one of our recent enrollees stated initially that he wanted to take both programs. This person's rationale was that he wants to know how the enemy works so he knows what to expect and how to defeat him. Friends, we cannot defeat Satan with man-made solutions. We can only defeat him with the sword of the Word of God.

At face value, knowing your enemy so you can defeat him sounds legitimate enough, but let us think this through. As children of God, we get the truth from the Word and get our leading and discernment from the Holy Spirit. Does it make any difference which deception the enemy throws at us? Greater is He who is in us than who is in the world. (1 John 4:4) In order to study a new-age or secular program, we would probably have to pay for it. We would at least have to buy their books. We would then be financially supporting the forces of evil that are at work to undermine our Lord and Savior. Given a choice, I would never deliberately support Satan's work.

Scripture is crystal clear about who we are to be connected to. The following scripture has often been used to discourage the marriage of a Christian to a non-believer. It has however, much further reaching directives. God's Word here is referring to every sort of partnership, contractual agreement, and yes, marriage.

> *"Be ye not unequally yoked together with unbelievers: for what fellowship hath righteousness with unrighteousness? And what communion hath light with darkness? And what concord hath Christ with Belial? Or what part hath he that believeth with an infidel? And what agreement hath the temple of God with idols? for ye are the temple of the living God; as God hath said, I will dwell in them, and walk in them; and I will be their God, and they shall be my people. Wherefore come out from among them, and be ye separate, saith the Lord, and touch not the unclean thing; and I will receive you. And will be a Father unto you, and ye shall be my sons and daughters, saith the Lord Almighty."* — II Corinthians 6:14-18 (KJV)

Occasionally some critics have suggested Christian training does not address the reality of the business world and strategic marketing. As Christians, our reality is different than that of an unbeliever. We are children of the most-high God. We have favor going out and favor coming in. Our training must be equal to our position. I agree that we should not settle for secular training. It would not be sufficient for us.

> *"Let them alone and disregard them; they are blind guides and teachers. And if a blind man leads a blind man, both will fall into a ditch."*
> — Matthew 15:14

As marketplace ministers we know coaching proficiency and marketing skills are not mutually exclusive. I know this personally because when God created me, he gave me a passion for business and marketing in addition to other talents. He did this so I could do business effectively as well as help others take their talents into the marketplace. God wants us to use our talents gainfully and avoid idleness.

Proverbs 19:15 says, *"Slothfulness casts one into a deep sleep, and the idle person shall suffer hunger."* It appears one who is disinclined to work or remains idle, will be hungry and broke. As coaches, the terms "hungry and broke" should never refer to us.

We need to honestly and ethically share and promote our services along-side other businesses in the marketplace. God has given us the tools we need with *Spirit-Led Marketing©*. This course begins with mindset and moves quickly into specific ways to reach those who need you. You can find details at http://pccca.org/slm/.

Deceptions in Christian Coaching

The Book of Revelations tells us in the last days there would be great deceptions. And indeed if we read all the promises made by new-age and secular coaching programs, we can see the enemy leading away well-meaning believers with promises of a panacea, a cure-all or solution for everything. New-age coaching is not a panacea. It is a step-by-step process of sinking deeper and deeper into the enemy's deception.

The Word tells us how we are to manage ourselves as Christian coaches.

> *"If you lay all these instructions before the brethren, you will be a worthy steward and a good minister of Christ Jesus, ever nourishing your own self on the truths of the faith and of the good (Christian) instruction which you have closely followed." — I Timothy 4:6*

We should not allow any secular or new-age strategies to infiltrate our practices lest we become confused or inadvertently confuse our clients. The Bible is very clear about this.

> *"But refuse and avoid irreverent legends (profane and impure and godless fictions, mere grandmothers' tales) and silly myths, and express your disapproval of them. Train yourself toward godliness (piety), [keeping yourself spiritually fit]." — I Timothy 4:7*

This leaves no doubt that we are to refuse every manner of coaching that does not line up with the Holy Bible. And we are to **express our disapproval** of them. It is also clear we are to train Christian life coaches on the truths of our Bible-based faith, and not mix in other fictions.

> *"For physical training is of some value (useful for a little), but godliness (spiritual training) is useful and of value in everything and in every way, for it holds promise for the present life and also for the life which is to come." — Timothy 4:8*

> "BLESSED (HAPPY, fortunate, prosperous, and enviable) is the man who walks and lives not in the counsel of the ungodly [following their advice, their plans and purposes], nor stands [submissive and inactive] in the path where sinners walk, nor sits down [to relax and rest] where the scornful [and the mockers] gather." — Psalms 1:1

This verse, the very first in the book of Psalms, is said to be the "preface psalm", the verse that is believed to be the foundation upon which the book of Psalms was laid forth. If you are ever challenged by others as to why you are maintaining a pure message for those you coach, the scripture above is all the support you need.

Non-Christian Coaching

Neuro Linguistic Programming (NLP)

NLP is not a Christian practice and should not be included as a Christian coach.

I recently received an email that read: "... I would like your opinion on the topic of Neuro-Linguistic Programming. A number of Christian life coaches are including this in their practice. To me this seems like it is depending less on the Lord and more on self, but I would like your opinion on the topic. Thank you. "

These days as I am sure you are aware, there are a lot of people who consider themselves Christian, who do all sorts of things. It is a shame and it is misleading to put it mildly. The truth of the matter is, NLP is an **apostate** practice, therefore *not* a Christian practice. Nothing in the Word of God supports it. Authentic Christian life coaches rely on the Holy Spirit to lead them and their client, not man-made manipulation and trickery.

Hypnosis

Hypnosis is used to change behavior of people in a relaxed, uninhibited and highly suggestible state. It causes a person to focus on the situation at hand rather than anything else around them.

Anything that gets in the way of the Holy Spirit revealing knowledge and wisdom to us is a form idolatry, which of course the first and second commandments speak against. We are not to put anything or anyone before God and we are not to make ourselves a graven idol. Put in plain words, we are not to make anyone or anything more important or give them priority over God.

> *"We are not to make anyone or anything more important or give them priority over God."*

As a Christian coach, let us say your client wants you to coach them to get a new job. That sounds wonderful until you find out the job the client wants would require him to work on Sunday and he would miss church every Sunday. If you coach a person to achieve this goal, would you be coaching them to disobey the first and fourth commandments? Remember, anything that has priority over God is an idol, regardless of whether it is a person, a thing, or an event.

EXERCISE

Could you coach the person above? If so, explain the terms in the section provided and how you would proceed.

_____
_____
_____
_____
_____

Christian Coaching and Compromise

Compromise is not viewed as a problem in any other type of coaching besides Christian coaching. In fact compromise is often seen as a solution and positive outcome in secular coaching.

As Christian coaches, we are to live our lives without compromising our faith principles. God will send us clients when He is sure we have the spiritual maturity to stand up for what we believe, no matter what. The most dangerous thing we can do is make it acceptable to add ungodly influences into our coaching strategies.

> "No one can serve two masters; for either he will hate the one and love the other, or he will stand by and be devoted to the one and despise and be [a]against the other. You cannot serve God and mammon ([b]deceitful riches, money, possessions, or [c]whatever is trusted in)." — Matthew 6:24
>
> "BLESSED (HAPPY, fortunate, prosperous, and enviable) is the man who walks and lives not in the counsel of the ungodly [following their advice, their plans and purposes], nor stands [submissive and inactive] in the path where sinners walk, nor sits down [to relax and rest] where the scornful [and the mockers] gather. — Psalms 1:1
>
> "Jesus said to him, No one who puts his hand to the plow and looks back [to the things behind] is fit for the kingdom of God." — Luke 9:62

SIX

Successful Coaches and Training

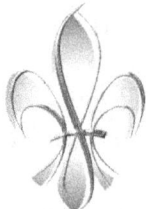

God has called us to achieve excellence and balance in our lives. Successful coaches have certain traits in common that help them attain and maintain distinction and stability. Let us take a look at what those characteristics are:

- Uncompromising personal faith (necessary attribute for all *Christian* coaches) This means you are unapologetically a Christian. You are not afraid to speak about your faith, what it means, and offer your personal testimony if called upon.

- Knowing in your heart you are called into this profession (necessary for all *Christian* Coaches)
- Highly attuned listening skills
- Common sense, practical wisdom
- Ability to address a variety of situations quickly
- Not judgmental
- Ability to ask powerful questions
- Ability to share inklings and observations at the appropriate time
- Honesty and integrity
- A positive world-view
- Great communication skills
- Organized and punctual. (You have to walk your talk.)

Take a look at this list again and review how many of the attributes fit you. Many coaches do not arrive at coaching with every single item met, but this will give you an idea of things you need to make sure are in place as you grow as a Christian life coach. Your CCLC or Certified Christian Life Coach training at PCCCA coaches you to overcome your personal challenges so you feel confident about living the life you will coach others to achieve.

COACH TRAINING ESSENTIALS

Why Get Certified?

I am often asked why Christian life coaches need to be certified. My answer is that they don't. However there are some very important reasons those intending to coach should receive this education.

As Christians, we understand the Word tells us to do everything as unto the Lord. Would we want to give God anything but the best? If you agree that as a Christian life coach, your clients and God deserve your best, the only way to give your best is to learn as much as possible about your profession and keep learning continually. In the 25th book of Matthew where we read the Parable of the Talents, we learn that each servant received talents according their own ability. While we don't have control over what others do, we do have opportunities to increase our own abilities. We should take every opportunity to learn and grow into the coach that God has designed us to be.

The second reason is to validate your skills, primarily to yourself, as a professional Christian life coach. Most coaches are unsure of themselves until they have gained some coaching experience and are seeing progress. Your training should give you the opportunity to be coached and to coach others in order to gain experience. We added a practicum to help you gain this experience.

There is potential for legal issues to crop up when one has not been trained. They would not understand the profession and boundaries of our practice. There is the danger someone could unknowingly impinge upon the counseling profession and end up in litigation or investigation for counseling without license or ordination. Additionally, it hurts the clients and the industry as a whole to have incompetent coaches.

You will see remarkable transformations along the way, both personally and professionally. New coaches would be missing a wonderful and remarkable facet of their professional potential without this training.

Questionable Value of Accreditation

For any who are new to this realm, accreditation is what a school may or may not have and certification is what an individual may or may not have.

It should be noted that accreditation is not required. Accreditation in coaching does *not* provide a measure of whether the courses are worthy. It is *not* a statement whether the faculty and staff have passed muster. For those who are unfamiliar with this area, you may wish to read "The Truth about Coaching School Accreditation" (Hilton-Goode) by Emery Hilton-Goode. Hilton-Goode states that accreditation is primarily a marketing ploy to draw in students to member schools and is also used to dissuade students from enrolling in schools that are not part of their organization.

Peer Resources, an unbiased coach training consortium from British Columbia, Canada, tells that coaching school accreditation does not mean one school is better than another. Rey Carr, president of Peer Resources states, "Visitors should note that 'accreditation' in the coaching field at present has a number of troubling aspects, including its lack of wide-spread acceptance, conflicts of interests between reviewers and some rated schools, minimal reporting of results, and questionable or vague criteria. While accreditation typically means the school has been reviewed by an external source, it does not necessarily mean that 'non-accredited schools' provide less value or poorer quality programs. Check with each school as to how it does assess the quality of its program and services," is the recommendation about accreditation according to the Peer website (Resources).

Some years ago, I was asked to serve on a council for a credentialing organization that accredits Christian schools and colleges in behavioral studies. A criterion was compiled by which Christian life coaching and counseling schools would be accredited. It is exciting to see Godly oversight where once there had primarily been secular and new-age organizations.

> "*T*raining contrary to your beliefs will plant seeds of doubt about your own faith.
>
> This is not a good place to be coaching from."
>
>

One of the foundational beliefs for accreditation is that the Christian coaching or counseling program encourages students to remain true to their faith. If they are asked to coach non-Christians, they may do so as long as the goals of the client do not conflict with their own biblically-based values. For transparency, they are encouraged to make sure the non-Christian clients understand the coaches' world-view is Christian. Why is this important? First, as Christians we cannot serve two masters (man and God). Second, we cannot promote a lifestyle in conflict with our own beliefs and the client should know to expect that.

I once received a phone call from a prospective Christian life coaching student, asking whether she should hide her faith from a non-Christian client.

I was astounded and asked where she came up with this concept. The woman then told me she had spoken with one of the leaders of another Christian coach training program (which by the way, is secularly accredited) and was told that for all practical purposes, when you enter the coaching relationship with a non-Christian, you are to leave your faith at the door. Her opinion was paraphrased here since I do not know her exact words.

This goes back to an authenticity issue for the coach and questions why the client hired this particular coach in the first place. If the coach cannot be counted on to be genuine with their client, what kind of relationship do they have? Can we agree that no trust can be built on a shallow and disingenuous relationship? And when there is no trust, can there be a true relationship at all? Of what value would such coaching be?

Christians and Secular Training

As Christian life coaches, it is important for us to have proper training so we can provide professional services with excellence. Christ calls us to a level of excellence in every aspect of our lives, personally and professionally. We are ambassadors for His Kingdom, and it is incumbent upon us to take our training seriously.

Based on my experience as a master Christian coach trainer, the belief systems of the coach training program should line up with the world-view of the coach, rather than with the beliefs of those that the student may eventually coach. If the program you study is incompatible with your beliefs, you will only become frustrated and morally conflicted. Training contrary to your beliefs will plant seeds of doubt about your own faith. This is not a good place to be coaching from.

The process of coaching is created, then facilitated by what the coach brings to the table. Coaches must be free to be themselves. If not, the relationship would become phony and the results would be skewed. Consequently the relationship that forms between the coach and client would remain superficial and insincere.

The Bible tells us (Matthew. 6:33) to seek first God's Kingdom and His righteousness, and everything else will be added unto us. That means, if we seek God and His Word first, then we will receive everything else we want and need... including clients!

I always tell students that God sends us those clients who need what we have to offer. The greater and more diverse our abilities, the more clients we are able to help. This is why we created training in so many Christian coaching specialties with more to come. Then because I saw so many students enrolling in one class after another, we recently added Course Bundles to provide savings. You can find more information about course bundles at http://pccca.org/course-bundles/.

SEVEN

Faith, Scripture and Communication

I believe that unless we understand the foundation of beliefs upon which Christian life coaching is based we will fail to grasp the effectiveness, power, and revelation available to us.

The most important foundational belief is that Jesus Christ is our Lord and Savior. Christian life coaching cannot occur without agreement to this fact. Secondarily, Jesus came that we might have life and have it in abundance. The scripture absolutely supports this.

The third foundational belief is that Jesus Christ is our Savior and He came to give us life everlasting as well as abundance here on earth. Christian life coaches believe that what we have and what we consequently receive is limited by how much we are willing to believe God. So the question arises:

HOW BIG IS YOUR GOD?

I use "your God" because I want God to become very personal for you here. We are not just talking about God up there, out there, somewhere. I am talking about the living God, through the Holy Spirit, who resides inside each one of us. Consider for yourself: What is MY God able to do? That is right — what is MY God able to do?

The Bible says we have not because we ask not. So, if everything else in our life is in order and if we are seeking the kingdom first and HIS righteousness, then Matthew 6:33 tells us everything else will be added unto us. What part of everything are we lacking? What are we confessing? How are we confessing it?

> *"How big is YOUR God?"*

See, Christian life coaching addresses these things. It uses scripture as the basis for what we believe. Then it takes the Word and applies it to our contemporary life. And that is as it should be, because God is the same yesterday, today, and tomorrow. Anything else may change but our God remains the same.

Because God does not change, true Christian life coaching will also never change as it is based on Holy Scripture. This is very exciting to me because the same biblical basis for coaching I teach today, is suitable to teach among generations to come.

Dr. Florine Milligan, BS, MSE in Counseling, a pastor who holds Certifications in Administration, TQM, Anger Management, and Master Christian Life Coaching, describes how Christian life coaches must also understand the position, abilities, and part that the Holy Spirit has in our life's journey (Milligan, 2006).

"As a wife, mother, educator, counselor, business partner, and now pastor, I have always had a desire to help people with life skills and spiritual development. I have found Christian life coaching to be the avenue to helping people find their God-given purpose and destiny for life.

The uniqueness of Christian life coaching vs. secular coaching is the dynamics of the power of the Holy Spirit as He directs, leads, and guides the coach in motivating the client to take ownership of the process of seeking God for His divine purpose and destiny for one's life.

Luke 12:12 says, *"For the Holy Ghost shall teach you in the same hour what ye ought to say."* That is powerful and convincing when coaching!! That 'rhema' word allows the coach-client relationship to be established with genuineness and power and thus providing a positive platform for the client to be successful in knowing their calling or defined directions.

My passion for Christian life coaching has intensified as I have gone through this training with such a dynamic coach as Dr. Bush. May God continue to bless Christian life coaching and its trainers and coaches."

THE HOLY SPIRIT'S PART

As you may be aware, various denominations, preachers, and churches offer varying amounts of emphasis on, or information about the Holy Spirit. It was not until I was over 30, that I came to understand that the Holy Spirit actually had a purpose. I had been raised in a Lutheran church as a child and then attended a Presbyterian church from age 20 to 30. In the particular congregations I attended, the Holy Ghost was part of the Apostles' Creed but rarely otherwise mentioned. After I no longer attended the Lutheran church, I heard they had experienced a church split because some "radical" believers had experienced a charismatic revival. It remained a mystery to me for many years.

Once I understood the role of the Holy Spirit and experienced His benefits, that connection with God I had been searching for my entire life was complete. Perhaps you or someone you know has had a similar experience, but until I became better acquainted with the Holy Spirit and the part He wants to have in my life, I felt that an indescribable *something* was missing.

Gary R. Collins, Ph.D., in his book *The Biblical Basis of Christian Counseling for People Helpers* (Gary R. Collins, 2001), put it this way saying, "... many people believe the Holy Spirit should mainly be left for hand-clapping charismatics and has little relevance for 'regular' Christians." Nothing could be further from the truth.

Just like God is the Father and Jesus Christ is His Son, the Holy Spirit is part of the triune God. The Holy Spirit is alive and lives inside each believer, only some people are unaware of this. Others are in denial about it or do not believe the Holy Spirit has a significant role in our lives today.

The Holy Spirit has come to be our helper, comforter and advocate, even counselor. The author, Gary Collins, states that as God may appear to be far away and Jesus Christ may seem to be removed from us because He lived on earth so long ago, the Holy Spirit is here today, right now, working in our life, our relationships and in every other aspect. Yes, the Holy Spirit even wants to have a part in our Christian life coaching relationships.

The Holy Spirit's Attributes

The author, Collins, states that the Holy Spirit has characteristics of personhood, and you can see this when looking closely at biblical references.

The Bible shows us that the Holy Spirit has similar traits to people. He has self-awareness, referring to Himself as "I" and "me" in the Bible. He has intelligence. He has a will. (I Corinthians 2:10-12 and I Corinthians 12:11) He has feelings and emotions and by our actions, we can bring him joy, grief or sorrow. We also read in the Bible that the Holy Spirit does things that people do. He teaches (John 14:26), convicts people of guilt and sin (John 16:7-9), intercedes for believers (Romans 8:26), and gives testimony (Romans 8:16). The way Paul wrote about the Holy Spirit, we can conclude that He has qualities and capabilities that are similar to those found in people.

We also read in the Bible that the Holy Spirit can be treated as people are sometimes treated. He can be lied to (Acts 5:3), resisted (Acts 7:51), insulted (Hebrews 10:29), and at other times obeyed (Acts 10:19-21).

Because the Holy Spirit has qualities like a person, He naturally becomes an integral part of the coaching relationship for the believing Christian life coach.

THE IMPORTANCE OF WORLD-VIEW IN COACHING

Secular coaching philosophies try to eliminate the coach's worldview, because the entire coaching relationship is intended to be based on the desires that the client finds from within. The coach is not supposed to work from a set of values or standards.

Christian life coaching is quite different. Clients hire a Christian life coach because they share a similar world-view. We as Christians are supposed to hold each other accountable, to exhort, encourage, and edify each other.

A Christian life coaching relationship would not exist in the absence of values or standards.

What then is a world-view and why is it important?

A worldview is how we think about people, evaluate issues, and create solutions. In order for it to be useful, it must help us make sense of life and the challenges imposed by life.

As a Christian life coach, we need to examine our world-views and make sure they are clear, rational, and biblically sound. Why? Because if we cannot articulate and role-model our views, we will have trouble making sense to our clients. We need to see whether our worldviews will stand the test of time. Can we live by them? Can we coach by them? If our worldview is not logical or based on the realities of life, then it is probably not much use to us or anyone else for that matter. Christian life coaches need to know what they believe and why they believe it.

LET GOD OUT OF THE BOX

Most of us have heard the expression "think outside the box." By that we mean we need to be more creative in our planning. We need to believe conventional methods are not necessarily the answer. We need to have the courage to think, research, discover, and devise new ways of thinking and doing things. It is frustrating to many of us, who believe in a God who knows no limits or boundaries, that some of us still hold on to ideas like:

> "... my husband, Evan, suggested we not only think 'outside the box', but rather that we 'get rid of the box altogether!'"

- "Well, God wouldn't do that these days. That was back in the Bible times."
- "Oh, I couldn't do that. We never did it that way before."
- "So and so might not understand or, might not like it"
- "I just couldn't."

For as long as I can remember, the word "impossible" has not been in my vocabulary. The only area the word "impossible" applies is where God intervenes or says "no." Being out of the will of God might well make something impossible. But if God says it, I believe it. Imagine how liberating it would be for someone to begin to believe that just about anything is possible. How awesome.

Someone reading this and knowing of my upbringing might wonder how I arrived at my faith. I certainly did not start out thinking this way. I grew up in a home where my mother told me not to hope for much so that I would not be disappointed when it did not materialize. That way of thinking never did suit me well or feel right.

I would not describe myself as an optimist necessarily or someone who looks at life through rose-colored glasses. Rather, I have preferred to consider myself a realist. I have lived long enough that I have known tragedy. I understand loss, poverty, abuse, neglect, and more.

But, I have seen more miracles than most people do in a lifetime. I have seen my daughter physically healed as a child, before my very eyes. I also know how God can suddenly intervene in a life and change everything. I know the power of faith. I have witnessed how a person's obedience, diligence, and steadfastness can transform their life because these attributes changed my life when I applied them.

The Bible tells us that what God will do for one person, He will do for another. Therefore I know that if God did this for me, He can do it for you. Are you ready?

> *"The Bible tells us that what God will do for one person, He will do for another."*

While discussing the box theory recently and how some people are held back by limited thinking, my husband, Evan, suggested we not only think "outside the box", but rather that we "get rid of the box altogether!"

With Christian life coaching, we can get rid of the box and man-imposed limitations. We can start living in as much abundance as we are willing to believe God will provide.

> *What does all this mean and how should we communicate with others now that we understand the faith and scripture component? Does anything need to change?*

Is it possible for a Christian life coach to come across as too overbearing about faith? Is it possible to be overly spiritual or too Christian? The Apostle Paul encourages us to become very aware of who our audience is and speak to them in terms they can understand. He recommends we remain relevant to those we are around so we can win them to Christ. But how do we do this?

Master Christian Life Coach and PCCCA coach trainer, Todd Miller wrote an extraordinarily thought-provoking article about the need for Christian coaches and all believers for that matter, to be aware of how we communicate with others so we don't instead, lose them.

Paul said he became all things to all men in order to save them.

> *"and to the Jews I became as a Jew, that I might win Jews; to those who are under the law, as under the law, that I might win those who are under the law; to those who are without law, as without law (not being without law toward God, but under law toward Christ), that I might win those who are without law; to the weak I became as weak, that I might win the weak. I have become all things to all men, that I might by all means save some."*
> — *1 Cor. 9:20-22 NKJV*

"Several years ago," explained Todd, "a friend of mine decided to pursue an education in the culinary arts. One night we ended up discussing salt. I don't remember how the conversation started. I probably grabbed the salt shaker and almost ruined his perfectly seasoned meal. In any case, he told me that the purpose of salt is to bring out the flavor of the food, to enhance it. If you taste the salt, then it's too salty."

"I chewed on his low sodium comment for a while, but it didn't fully sink in until my daughter was baking some cookies and had to add salt to the recipe," continued Todd. "Wait a minute. Cookies are sweet. Yet they have salt in them. Leave the salt out next time you bake some cookies and see how they turn out. Salt brings out the flavor. It enhances the flavor, but you shouldn't taste the salt."

"In the Certified Christian Life Coach training at PCCCA, a module is dedicated to scripture verses and contemplating what they mean to us as Christians. One of those verses is Matthew 5:13, 'You are the salt of the earth, but if salt has lost its taste, how shall its saltiness be restored? It is no longer good for anything except to be thrown out and trampled under people's feet.' This verse took on a new, fuller meaning for me after my conversation with my chef friend. It gave me a better understanding of our mission as Christians. More importantly, it made me ask if it is possible to be too salty even as a Christian."

"Most of us have that friend who is just a little too much, even for other Christians. When you ask them how their day is going, they give you a Bible verse and quote book, chapter, and verse. It's as if they cannot have a normal conversation. Every word that comes out of their mouth is covered in salt, and eventually, you just can't stomach it anymore. Imagine what might be like for someone who is not a believer, is a struggling believer, or has been hurt by a previous experience with the church. Some people have theological high blood pressure, yet we're just piling on the salt."

"When we read Jesus' words in the Holy Bible, we do not see one who is regurgitating scripture to people and piling on the verses. I do believe that Jesus taught scripture directly, but the gospels show a Jesus who shares scripture through stories. And when he does mention scripture more directly, he states it as a fact, as truth, without quoting book, chapter, and verse. This is what we should do also. 'Truly, truly, I say to you, whoever believes in me will also do the works that I do...' (John 14:12). He tells us to do what he did. Don't even worry about the next part of this verse until you get the first part down."

> *"Salt brings out the flavor. It enhances the flavor, but you shouldn't taste the salt."*
> — Todd Miller, MCLC

Todd gives three simple tips to help you avoid being too salty:

- **Test before you salt** – Find out a little about the person you are talking to. Have a regular conversation about their job, the weather, or just life in general. Try to answer questions such as: Are they a believer? Are they an atheist? Are they a Muslim? Have they had a bad experience?
- **Offer a low salt version** – If you know someone is not a believer, try using a secular film to discuss theological topics. For example, *The Last Witch Hunter* is a great movie to use to talk about good and evil.
- **Worry about flavor** – Try to just leave the person and/or place better for having been there. In Acts, Paul tells his shipmates that they will be saved just because Paul is there. Be like that.

"We don't need to prove we are Christian in every conversation," concludes Todd. "We need to show them how we treat others by how we think and by how we live. Love God. Love your neighbor and don't over salt it."

I believe the key is balance. There are times as Christian coaches and in life, we find ourselves in settings where for one reason or another, we need to communicate in a way that shares the love of Jesus with others, yet we may not be led to begin a discussion about faith. This is an intersection where lives can be saved and lives can be lost if handled incorrectly. It was helpful to me to see the balanced way Todd dealt with this sensitive topic.

Now that we have addressed faith, scripture and the way we communicate, what are your thoughts?

Action Step:

On a sheet of paper, draw two columns. At the top of the left column, put the word SITUATION and at the top of the left column, put MY RESPONSE. Then on the left, list common situations in your life where you might be tempted to be "too salty". On the right column, give lower sodium responses.

Finally, how did it feel to perform this exercise?

I recommend we pray and listen for insight and wisdom when communicating with others. Lean in to the answer you receive from God. When you pray, ask for revelation. Then remain still to allow the Holy Spirit to lead you in what to say and when.

EIGHT

Coachable or Uncoachable?

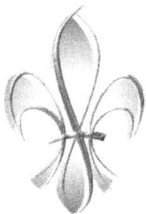

Unlike what some might think, not everyone is coachable and those who are, might not always be coachable to the same degree. For anyone who wishes to coach another, there are three elements that must exist for coaching to be successful.

THREE CRITERIA FOR SUCCESSFUL COACHING

- There must be one or more areas of someone's life that they want to improve.
- The person must be willing to allow someone else (such as the coach) into the process.

○ The person has to be agreeable to making some changes, meaning do or think about things differently than in the past. We all know that if we keep doing what we are doing, we will keep getting the same results.

> *"We should only coach our clients to achieve that which lines up with the Word of God."*
>
>

Let's examine the criteria more closely.

First, if there is not something in a person's life they want to make better or care about enough to want improvement or change, any effort made by the coach will most likely be useless and avail no measurable results.

Second, in order for coaching to be successful, the person being coached has to be willing to include the coach in the process. Coaching implies a relationship between two people; one of whom is the coach and the other is the person being coached. If there is no relationship, there can be no coaching.

Third, the person being coached needs to be agreeable to changing something in order for small changes to occur, even if it is only the way they *think* about the issue. The more the person being coached is willing to do, the greater the transformation will be. Alternatively, if the person being coached will not make any changes in thinking or actions, no progress can be made.

Having trained thousands of coaches from novice to advanced, I have observed that one of the primary mistakes new coaches make is selecting practicum clients who have the worst problems they can find. New coaches seem to think that if a person is really bad off, they will benefit far more dramatically from coaching. While a transformation may be greater if this type of coaching is successful, the odds of success in these cases are slim.

The reason is that problems do not develop overnight and poor choices do not suddenly impact a person's life. The people we find with severe problems have generally been in those situations for a significant amount of time. Problems that do not occur suddenly usually cannot be solved quickly.

People in these situations are usually where they are because of decisions they have made. Perhaps they truly are victims of circumstances. If this is the case, will they quickly drop a victim mentality and become a coachable overcomer? It is certainly possible, but usually some counseling or therapy will be needed before they will become truly coachable. It will take time.

Nearly all of us began studying coaching because we want those around us to enjoy a richer, more fulfilling life. As Christians, we believe that obedience to God's plan for our life will bring us the greatest fulfillment, blessing, and happiness. Therefore, we also set desire for alignment with God's plan as a criteria for those we coach. We should only coach our clients to achieve that which lines up with the Word of God. Anything else might present a conflict with our values, morals, ethics, or faith. Additionally, there are more specific criteria to determine whether a person is coachable and whether the situation is appropriate for coaching. The following information will help you determine the likelihood that an agenda can be accomplished through coaching.

COACHABLE OR UNCOACHABLE?

That is the Question.

Below you will find characteristics of coachable clients and situations and those that are uncoachable. You will waste a lot of time and energy if you don't understand the difference.

Characteristics of a COACHABLE client and situation

- The desired outcome must be **in line with the Word of God**.
- The **timing must be led of the Holy Spirit**. In other words, both the coach and client must feel secure (discernment) that "now is the time" to proceed.
- The **client must have control** over their actions and options.

- The **client is in a place to be able to speak freely and confidentially** with the coach.
- The client has insight and i**s able to accurately describe the situation** and how their actions might affect this situation.
- The **client is willing to risk doing things differently** in order to achieve the change.
- The **change must be measurable** in a way that can be communicated to the coach.

Characteristics of an UNCOACHABLE client and situation

- The **client does not have control** over their actions. (i.e. The client's superior will not allow a change in how things are done.)
- The **client is unable or unwilling to be truthful** about the situation.
- The **client is frightened about making a change** sufficiently to paralyze progress.
- The **client lacks a high level of interest** in seeing change occur.
- The **client thinks no action they take will make a difference** in the outcome (fatalism).
- The **client primarily wants to complain** about the situation without taking any action or responsibility for the outcome.
- The **client lacks follow through** to take agreed-upon actions to bring about change.
- The **client is not willing to take a close look at the situation** and/or options.
- The actions required must be taken by someone other than the client.

SHOULD SOMEONE IN COUNSELING ALSO HAVE A COACH?

The decision about whether or not it is in the best interest of a client in counseling to also be coached should be made by the client's counselor or therapist so as not to interfere with clinical issues. I recommend coaches include a question on intake forms (or personal inventories / information sheets) inquiring whether the client is currently in counseling. It is important for coaches to know this so they can discuss the appropriateness of adding coaching to a client's life at that time with their counselor or therapist.

It should also be noted that without proper release forms signed by the client, the counselor or therapist may not be allowed to discuss the case with the coach due to confidentiality issues. There are some counselors or therapists who do not yet see the value of life coaching, or Christian life coaching to be specific. Those professionals are less likely to make a recommendation in favor of coaching. Our primary goal must be the client's wellbeing.

> *"Coaching should not attempt to take the place of counseling or other therapy."*
>
>

It is my recommendation that the prospective coach meet with and review the client's case with the counselor or therapist. However, if it is clear the counselor will not approve of adding a regimen of coaching, the coach should respect such an opinion. Coaching should not attempt to take the place of counseling or other therapy. A coach must always be aware of a prospective client's needs and refer them to another professional if their own expertise does not qualify them to work with that individual.

It should also be noted if you encounter someone who is not currently in counseling or therapy, but should be, a referral should be made immediately. It is always a good idea to become familiar with other professional services and service providers in your community so you can make a referral based on knowing to whom you are sending someone.

Having started as a Christian counselor many years prior to becoming a Christian life coach, I can attest that my clients progressed much faster when coaching was added to sessions than they did with traditional counseling techniques.

When we review the life of Jesus, we see that what He did was much more similar to today's version of coaching than it was like contemporary counseling. We don't read about Jesus Christ sitting and listening to others rehash their past hurts and pains for hours on end, do we? Most certainly not. What we do witness is Jesus asking others how he may help them and then assisting them. He also adds "according to your faith, may it be done unto you."

This tells us that what we receive will be in direct proportion to what we are willing to believe for. Doesn't this bring us full circle back to the question, "How big is your God?"

Opt for Great vs. Good

Laurie Beth Jones, in her phenomenally successful book, *Jesus Life Coach* (Jones, 2004), discusses leaving behind what is good in favor of what is great. She introduces the concept of "planned abandonment" which means that you are able to say "no" to all that glitters and discern what truly shines. Jones says once you understand the difference, you are on your way to fulfillment.

The author, Jones, tells the story of Mary and Martha from Luke 10:38-42 (NIV) where Jesus told Martha that Mary had chosen what is better when she left the kitchen duties to listen to Jesus. The story tells of planned abandonment by Mary. She decided to let lesser things go in order to choose the higher part. Jesus practiced planned abandonment.

Likewise, during his CCLC coach training, Pastor Brian Koch from Reading, PA, reminded me (paraphrased) the worst enemy of excellence was "good enough". Good enough causes us to settle. God's word is NEVER about compromising our aim for excellence.

Believe for Specifics

Having faith is imperative. Removing barriers, obstacles, and limitations is important. But how do we know when our faith for what God will do is coming to life? We know it when we are willing to believe for specific things. Right here, right now, we are living the life we believe we are entitled to live. For better or for worse, we are where we should be, based on what we believe.

Let us get specific. What is something you are tolerating in your life? Why do you think you continue to put up with it? I believe it is because of an internal script we have about how things have always been and how things will likely always be. Christian life coaching helps us get specific about changing what needs to be changed so that we can begin living in abundance like the King's kids we are.

Asking the Right Questions

Some Christians are drawn to life coaching because they have long been sought out for sharing sound advice. They love to help others and voice their opinions openly. These people believe they will make sensational Christian life coaches. Most of them are surprised to learn that Christian life coaching is not the same as professional advice-giving.

Brought down to the simplest of concepts, Christian life coaches traditionally do not give advice. What we do is ask the right questions so our client or person we are coaching comes up with their own right answers. In addition to this, we need to be familiar with the Word. If our client strays off track with what is biblically required of Christians, we are there to help them make a course correction in thinking or doing. Particularly gifted Christian life coaches are so in tune with the Holy Spirit during their sessions with clients that they speak freely about what they discern by the Spirit.

Some time back, I recall sharing with my husband, how sometimes in a session, I say things I was not even thinking. I once strayed from my session focus momentarily to consider I was hungry for lunch. A moment later, words came from me that supported and exhorted my client on their path. The client was amazed at how insightful I was. At that point, I knew it was not me. It was the Holy Spirit speaking through me. I was but the vessel.

Referral to a Mental Health Professional

Although not typical, there are times when we as coaches realize someone needs to be referred to a counselor or other mental health professional. It might be someone you have been working with or a new or prospective client. Listed below are common signs that a referral to a mental health professional needs to be made instead of proceeding with coaching. This list is neither exhaustive nor complete, but includes the basic signs you need to be aware of. A referral should be made when the person:

- is exhibiting a decline in their ability to experience pleasure or is becoming increasingly sad, hopeless or helpless.
- has intrusive thoughts or is unable to concentrate or focus.
- sleeps too much or not enough. Might exhibit more than usual trouble getting to sleep or often wakes up and is unable to return to sleep. Also, be aware if the person seems to be sleeping excessively.
- has a marked and ongoing increase or decrease in appetite.
- experiences guilt because others have suffered or died.
- has feelings of despair or hopelessness.
- is being hyper alert or excessively tired.
- has increased irritability or outbursts of anger.

While none of the above signs indicate something is definitely, seriously wrong, a coach is not trained to diagnose or assess whether mental health issues exist. That must be left to a trained professional. (Note: If you have been trained and have the appropriate credentials to provide counseling or therapy, then a referral may not be necessary.)

How to Make the Referral

Making a referral to a mental health provider may be an uncomfortable conversation for a new coach, but I have found the following statement works best. Simply tell the individual, "I appreciate that you would like to work with me. However, I do not believe my skills as a coach are the right fit (or match) for you at this time. I would like to refer you to a couple others, who may be better equipped to assist you." If they ask why, tell them you are not qualified to help them in these areas and you want to be sure they get the assistance they need. I have yet to have anyone be offended at my sincere desire to help them by providing a referral. Then, have the referral information, including names and phone numbers, on hand.

Receiving Referrals from Counselors or Therapists

As I mentioned previously, as part of your new client information form, it is important you ask whether the prospective client is currently in counseling. Participating in counseling and coaching simultaneously is usually not a good idea as it can cause confusion for the client. But once counseling has been completed, there are cases where it is helpful for the former counseling patient to retain a coach. The purpose would be to help sustain positive, healthy behaviors. This type of work often isn't covered under an insurance plan's counseling benefits. Counseling centers may be a source of referrals for this type of client.

I recommend that you foster relationships with counselors in your area, particularly Christian counselors in private practice and at churches, so that if this sort of need arises, they may refer to you. Another source is school counselors. Christian schools have counselors who frequently make referrals. But just as often, public school counselors have taken my information to refer for cases when a family or student may want a coach from the same spiritual worldview.

Make sure your referral sources understand coaches work with healthy, functioning individuals. There are times counseling is not the best solution. If the person is generally healthy and just wants to overcome a situation or improve their life, coaching may be a positive alternative.

NINE

Ten Christian Coaching Proficiencies

The Christian coaching proficiencies in this section are ones every Christian coach should aspire to. Various coaching proficiencies have been developed by a variety of coaching organizations over the years to set performance standards, goals, and baselines. After training thousands of Christian coaches worldwide, I understand the importance of standardizing certain professional skills. Additionally, it is critical that the Ten Christian Coaching Proficiencies© agree with our biblical foundation and Christian world view. After each one, you will see scriptures on which that particular proficiency is based. An area for recording your personal notes is provided for each of the proficiencies listed.

1 – Inspire anointed conversation.

> "THE SPIRIT of the Lord God is upon me, because the Lord has anointed and qualified me to preach the Gospel of good tidings to the meek, the poor, and afflicted; He has sent me to bind up and heal the brokenhearted, to proclaim liberty to the [physical and spiritual] captives and the opening of the prison and of the eyes to those who are bound," — Isaiah 61:1

> "But it is God Who confirms and makes us steadfast and establishes us [in joint fellowship] with you in Christ, and has consecrated and anointed us [enduing us with the gifts of the Holy Spirit];" — II Corinthians 1:21

Inspiring conversation happens when God's anointing motivates or incites what is being said. The coach should listen to what the client is saying, what the Holy Spirit is revealing, and also to anything the client may leave unsaid. Ask the right questions, push for clarity, and share anything the Holy Spirit may be revealing to you. If something occurs to you that the client has not mentioned, ask the client's permission, to share your thoughts, ideas or observations. You might ask, "Do you mind if I share my thoughts about this?" or "May I share an idea that came to me?"

Key application:

Allow your clients to express themselves freely. Remain tuned into what the Holy Spirit may be revealing. Ask for specific details. Do not presume your client has already thought everything through. Your questions will help them explore and discover more.

_____

_____

_____

2 – Encourage awareness of God's plan.

> "And we desire that every one of you do shew the same diligence to the full assurance of hope unto the end: That ye be not slothful, but followers of

them who through faith and patience inherit the promises." — Hebrews 6:11-12 (KJV)

"I know thy works, that thou art neither cold nor hot: I would thou wert cold or hot. So then because thou art lukewarm, and neither cold nor hot, I will spew thee out of my mouth." — Rev. 3:15-16 (KJV)

"But if from there you will seek (inquire for and require as necessity) the Lord your God, you will find Him if you [truly] seek Him with all your heart [and mind] and soul and life." — Deut. 4:29

"Keep on asking and it will be given you; keep on seeking and you will find; keep on knocking [reverently] and [the door] will be opened to you." — Matthew 7:7-8

"But without faith it is impossible to please and be satisfactory to Him. For whoever would come near to God must [necessarily] believe that God exists and that He is the rewarder of those who earnestly and diligently seek Him [out]." — Hebrews 11:6

The more aware someone is about themselves, their calling and vision, the better choices they can make in their life. It is your job to help clients and students discover their gifts, callings, talents, wants, values, needs and visions for their own life and any potential ministry. The better informed a client is, the faster they move forward.

Key applications:

- Point to their unseen gifts / visions / aspirations.
- Help them see their way of thinking (or paradigm).
- Help them identify their source of motivation/energy.
- Administer a "Spiritual Gifts Test" if deemed appropriate.

_____

_____

_____

3 – Draw out excellence; let success happen.

"Trust (lean on, rely on, and be confident) in the Lord and do good; so shall you dwell in the land and feed surely on His faithfulness, and truly you shall be fed." — Psalm 37:3

"And I am convinced and sure of this very thing, that He Who began a good work in you will continue until the day of Jesus Christ [right up to the time of His return], developing [that good work] and perfecting and bringing it to full completion in you. — Philippians 1:6

When we can help the client become more self-aware and aware of their relationship to the Lord, we can show them biblically and practically, how they are called to greatness. We need to ask the client to think in larger terms and challenge them to raise the bar on their standards. We know that God never does things in a small way, so when we line up with His divine plan for our lives, we soon find ourselves involved with grander plans, programs and goals.

Key applications:

- Get clarity on the client's calling.
- Ask for higher standards.
- Ask the client to think in terms of a bigger plan.
- Prepare the client to follow the Lord's leading when they realize specifics.

___

___

4 – Demonstrate love and grace toward the client.

"For it is by free grace (God's unmerited favor) that you are saved ([a]delivered from judgment and made partakers of Christ's salvation) through [your] faith. And this [salvation] is not of yourselves [of your own doing, it came not through your own striving], but it is the gift of God;" — Ephesians 2:8

And the Child grew and became strong in spirit, filled with wisdom; and the grace (favor and spiritual blessing) of God was upon Him." — Luke 2:40

"And become useful and helpful and kind to one another, tenderhearted (compassionate, understanding, loving-hearted), forgiving one another [readily and freely], as God in Christ forgave you." — Ephesians 4:32

"THEREFORE, [there is] now no condemnation (no adjudging guilty of wrong) for those who are in Christ Jesus, who live [and] walk not after the

dictates of the flesh, but after the dictates of the Spirit. For the law of the Spirit of life [which is] in Christ Jesus [the law of our new being] has freed me from the law of sin and of death." — Romans 8:1-2

Learn to love your client regardless of their challenges and frustrations. We call this agape love, or Christ-like, unconditional love. This is part of our "love walk." **Read I Corinthians 13 and other biblical references to love.**

When the client feels loved, higher levels of trust occur. When there is greater trust, you can be more effective as their coach or mentor. Be real and authentic so that clients know you are totally there for them. When the Master Coach is at this point with the person being coached, the coaching becomes collaborative and light, not heavy.

Key application:

This type of coach or client relationship is prime for the Holy Spirit to start revealing more and more direction, information ... and the session will begin to flow under a new power.

___

___

5 – Optimize and Celebrate the Client's Efforts.

"Be strong, courageous, and firm; fear not nor be in terror before them, for it is the Lord your God Who goes with you; He will not fail you or forsake you." — Deuteronomy 31:6

"Be strong and courageous. Be not afraid or dismayed before the king of Assyria and all the horde that is with him, for there is Another with us greater than [all those] with him. With him is an arm of flesh, but with us is the Lord our God to help us and to fight our battles. And the people relied on the words of Hezekiah king of Judah." — II Chronicles 32:7-8

"Be alert and on your guard; stand firm in your faith ([a]your conviction respecting man's relationship to God and divine things, keeping the trust and holy fervor born of faith and a part of it). Act like men and be courageous; grow in strength!" — I Corinthians 16:13

An important reason for hiring a coach or working with one, is so the coach will support the client to achieve more in a shorter period of time than they would have done on their own. A masterful coach will bring about more and faster results by creating accountability. When the client feels accountable to the coach to take agreed-upon actions, they will have a stronger commitment.

Key applications:

- ○ Congratulate the client and then ask for an even higher standard.
- ○ Reinforce the client's thoughts of what is actually possible (because with God, nothing is impossible).
- ○ Raise the bar for your client's next action step. When the client knows we expect more, the client performs at a higher level.

"Increase your performance to meet higher standards, rather than lowering your standards to match the performance."

_____

_____

_____

6 – Don't presume you know. (Ask, then listen.)

"There was a certain man there who had suffered with a deep-seated and lingering disorder for thirty-eight years. When Jesus noticed him lying there [helpless], knowing that he had already been a long time in that condition, He said to him, Do you want to become well? [Are you really in earnest about getting well?" — John 5:5-6

When we ask our client questions, the client enjoys a new learning process. When they devise their answer, they learn more about themselves. After all, Christian coaches are called to help the client align more closely with God's plan. And how can you help the client find new and better ways of doing things if you do not ask substantive questions? Then listen closely for what they client says and what may be left unsaid. A by-product of this is that both the coach and client will learn more and get a better picture of what needs to be done.

Key applications:

- Ask for clarity about situations.
- Don't guess at what your client needs. Rather, ask him/her.
- Seek knowledge about interpersonal dynamics.
- Verify your understanding of the facts.

7 – Abate fear with confidence in God's divine purpose

"THE LORD is my Light and my Salvation–whom shall I fear or dread? The Lord is the Refuge and Stronghold of my life–of whom shall I be afraid?" — Psalm 27:1

"The fear of man brings a snare, but whoever leans on, trusts in, and puts his confidence in the Lord is safe and set on high." — Proverbs 29:25

"For God did not give us a spirit of timidity (of cowardice, of craven and cringing and fawning fear), but [He has given us a spirit] of power and of love and of calm and well-balanced mind and discipline and self-control." — II Timothy 1:7

As Christians we know God allows things to happen for reasons we do not understand. And we do not always see how He uses the most difficult of situations for good. But, as Christians, we know that God can and does use everything... the good and the bad for His great purpose.

Key application:

- Remind the client that God will never leave or forsake them.

8 – Pray for discernment about priorities.

"But seek (aim at and strive after) first of all His kingdom and His righteousness (His way of doing and being right), and then all these things taken together will be given you besides." — Matthew 6:33

"But even in case you should suffer for the sake of righteousness, [you are] blessed (happy, to be envied). Do not dread or be afraid of their threats, nor be disturbed [by their opposition]." — I Peter 3:14

Key application:

- We need to allow our clients to modify their goals as they themselves grow and get a better understanding of where God wants them and what God wants them to do.

Depending upon circumstances and new revelations, what is most important may be a moving target until someone gets in line with God during times when new visions are being birthed.

_____

_____

_____

9 – Improve communication skills.

"Let the words of my mouth and the meditation of my heart be acceptable in Your sight, O Lord, my [firm, impenetrable] Rock and my Redeemer." — Psalm 19:14

"Let your Yes be simply Yes, and your No be simply No; anything more than that comes from the evil one." — Matthew 5:37

"The mind of the wise instructs his mouth, and adds learning and persuasiveness to his lips." — Proverbs 16:23

"The mouths of the righteous (those harmonious with God) bring forth skillful and godly Wisdom, but the perverse tongue shall be cut down [like a barren and rotten tree]." — Proverbs 10:31

"Let no foul or polluting language, nor evil word nor unwholesome or worthless talk [ever] come out of your mouth, but only such [speech] as

is good and beneficial to the spiritual progress of others, as is fitting to the need and the occasion, that it may be a blessing and give grace (God's favor) to those who hear it." — Ephesians 4:29*

It is important to communicate clearly. Our explanations, questions, thoughts, tips, and methods need to be well organized. Our conversations need to reveal God to the client. Our writing needs to be motivational, inspirational, and of good quality. If the coach is not confident in their writing ability, they should hire an assistant who will proof the work prior to sending. There are many excellent free training resources on the internet. Research tips and training for writers. Then increase your writing ability as this will be an important asset to you as a coach.

Key applications:

- Communicate clearly.
- Keep questions, thoughts, and inspirations well organized.
- Become a skilled writer and speaker.

___

___

___

10 – Build supportive environments

"Then Peter and the apostles replied, We must obey God rather than men." — Acts 5:29

"For the time being no discipline brings joy, but seems grievous and painful; but afterwards it yields a peaceable fruit of righteousness to those who have been trained by it [a harvest of fruit which consists in righteousness—in conformity to God's will in purpose, thought, and action, resulting in right living and right standing with God]." — Hebrews 12:11

"But those who wait for the Lord [who expect, look for, and hope in Him] shall change and renew their strength and power; they shall lift their wings and mount up [close to God] as eagles [mount up to the sun]; they shall run and not be weary, they shall walk and not faint or become tired." — Isaiah 40:31

> "I know that whatever God does, it endures forever; nothing can be added to it nor anything taken from it. And God does it so that men will [reverently] fear Him [revere and worship Him, knowing that He is]."
> — Ecclesiastes 3:14

Our goal as Christian coaches is to help clients develop to the point where making the right choices and responding, as opposed to reacting, comes naturally, because they are seeking the Lord before any other thing. Coaching helps the client become more disciplined in their own life. We want clients to develop good habits. We know it is a lot easier for clients to accomplish goals when their action steps become second nature.

Key application:

- Encourage development of the following supportive environments:

    - Regular devotional time
    - Church family
    - Knowledge of God's word
    - Christian fellowship
    - Family and friends
    - Daily spiritual disciplines
    - Other _____

_____

_____

_____

REVIEW

Below are the **Ten Christian Coaching Proficiencies©**. Make sure you employ each of them during your coaching sessions.

1. **Inspire anointed conversation.**
2. **Encourage awareness of God's plan.**
3. **Draw out excellence; let success happen.**
4. **Demonstrate love and grace toward the client.**
5. **Optimize and celebrate the client's efforts.**
6. **Don't presume you know. (Ask, then listen.)**
7. **Abate fear with confidence in God's divine purpose.**
8. **Pray for discernment about priorities.**
9. **Improve communication skills.**
10. **Build supportive environments.**

TEN

Coaching Systems, Methods, or Models

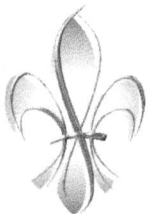

Coaches have long sought ways to categorize and systematize what we do in our coaching sessions. All coaches benefit from having procedures in place for the way in which they conduct coaching sessions.

Often times, these procedures have been termed "models," however, I find the term inadequate to describe what happens. A model is defined as "a preliminary work or construction that serves as a plan from which a final product is to be made (The Free Dictionary)"

When we provide coaching for someone, we are generally not experimenting with how to arrive at solutions. As professionals, we need to be able to chart a course. That makes me think perhaps "system" is a better word to describe the process we use.

A system is defined as "a method or set of methods for doing or organizing something" (The Free Dictionary). Now we are getting closer to what actually happens during coaching sessions.

> *"If we are unwilling to risk following as the Holy Spirit leads ... we stagnate as a coach and dishonor the God who put us here."*

I like the term "method" best, as a method is defined as "a means or manner of procedure, especially a regular and systematic way of accomplishing something" (www.thefreedictionary.com 8/15/09). But be aware that the terms systems, methods, or models are actually used interchangeably by many in the coaching industry.

The Benefit of Using Specific Methods

The greatest benefit of using a specific method for coaching is that the coach can have a more organized and less random way of helping their clients. The process is simplified and generalized to allow for optimum latitude in working with almost any client within the coach's niche or specialty.

Risk Moving to the Unknown or Suffer Stagnation

Frequently you will hear talk among coaches about competencies as barometers of our performance. Of course it is very important to be competent. It is even more imperative for Christians to perform with excellence. We must have skills and motivation in order to perform with these results. However, this presents us with a problem in expanding our expertise if we rigidly follow the same system.

If we are to grow, by necessity we will begin in a place of incompetence. And if we are never willing to step out and coach from a place of incompetence, it will be impossible for us to grow into our profession. If we are unwilling to risk following as the Holy Spirit leads, because it feels uncomfortable outside of what we have learned, then we stagnate as a coach and dishonor the God who put us here. Further, we will not be able to develop our own, unique brand of coaching.

Great coaching develops from experience gained over time. Without practice and stretching of our coaching muscles, we will be held back from ever achieving excellence.

> "Our faith has to be great enough that when we feel led to say something, we obediently deliver the message."
>
>

Additionally, if we are over attached to being competent, then we may only ever rise to a place we can perform adequately. But if we want to become great coaches, we must be willing to take some risks. We need to stretch beyond what is comfortable. The best way to describe this is that we need to **coach from faith**.

"Now faith is the substance of things hoped for, the evidence of things not seen." — Hebrews 11:1 (KJV)

In secular coaching, the coach places their faith in the client's ability to perform the next step toward achieving their goal, and to express their confidence in their client. After all, that is what partnering is about. Both the coach and client bring faith to their coaching relationship or partnership. The client has faith the coach will help them achieve more. The coach has faith in the client's willingness and ability to take the next, agreed-upon step.

In Christian coaching, we place our faith in God, who will lead both the coach and the client with His Holy Spirit. Christian life coaching is most powerful when both the coach and client remain open to the leading of the Holy Spirit in coaching sessions and in their individual lives. Coaches need to avoid getting hung up on particular methods and systems in order to not risk missing what God may be showing us about a particular situation. If we opt to use a specific method, we should still remain open to what the Holy Spirit will bring to our consciousness as we are coaching.

The discipline can be likened to listening to our client with our ears and listening for God's instructions with our heart. When this happens, our mind sorts through the messages, and then we share an anointed message with our client — the message God has for them in that time.

I frequently hear coaches I have trained describe times they suddenly felt led to say something to a client. The thought seemingly came out of nowhere. Yet, when the coach spoke the words, the client knew this was a special word intended just for them at that time. I have personally witnessed clients respond with great surprise or near disbelief, with joy or tears.

Our faith has to be great enough that when we feel led to say something we obediently deliver the message. God's words will always accomplish their intent. The duty is ours to deliver the message, but the results belong to God. This is a theme you will see throughout Christian coaching.

We cannot allow ourselves to get so wrapped up in worry about the results that we fail to deliver the message. We must consciously abandon any fear of coaching from faith.

What are common fears we may encounter?

- What if the client gets mad at us?
- What if the client fires us? (And we need the money!)
- What if we look stupid?
- What if we missed God?
- What will others think?

Some of the above may look familiar. Maybe you have experienced one or more of these fears. I have had most of the above but delivered the messages regardless. Interestingly, if you look again at the list of fears, you will notice that they all have something to do with the coach's ego or agenda. Reminder: It's not about you, coach!

We must coach fearlessly, from a position of faith. We must love our client more than our perceived self-image. God's word tells us that perfect love casts out all fear.

> *"There is no fear in love; but perfect love casteth out fear: because fear hath torment. He that feareth is not made perfect in love."* — I John 4:18 (KJV)

Why do clients want to work with a coach — particularly a Christian coach? They desire to partner with the coach because the coach brings hope of change. The coaching relationship then becomes alive with hope and anticipation of improvement. The client is motivated by the coach's unwavering faith. They feel encouraged by the coach's love.

In summary:

Coach from faith

Coach from hope

Coach from love

THE SPIRIT-LED F-L-O-W COACHING METHOD©

How does this method work? Below each header is a description of that step.

Follow the leading of the Holy Spirit.
Prior to the coaching session, prepare by praying for the Holy Spirit to give you wisdom and discernment.

Let God have control in your sessions.
Always follow God's agenda rather than your own.

Open up to revelations as led by the Holy Spirit.
Listen and share revelation and confirmation.

Witness & acknowledge the greatness of God in solutions and strategies He imparts.

The great take-away from each session is the testimony you have about how God's power, love and mercy manifested. (Keep these confidential unless the client has given you written permission to share their story.)

This is the model many of my colleagues and I flow in. Why? We do this because most likely we "flow" this way in every other aspect of our life.

> *"We can also be sure that this one method (F-L-O-W) always brings the exact results God has ordered."*

We can be sure that this one method always brings the exact results God has ordered. It does not get any better or more powerful than that! The Holy Spirit was sent to be our ultimate counselor and aid.

Our God is the Alpha and the Omega, the beginning and the end. God owns all of the resources and His are the results. We are here to manage the resources and be obedient to do as He says.

Therefore, there is **nothing** man can add to or improve on for God. God has already completed His way of doing things. You just need to learn what His Word promises. He already knows the plans He has for us. His will and His timing are perfect.

What can we, as coaches, pretend to add to God?

ELEVEN

Values-Based Life Design

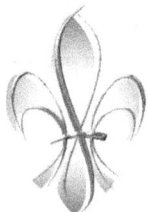

What are values? Values are your beliefs about what is most important to you. Once you are aware of your values, you want to live by them and life does not feel right unless you are living by them. In order to discover your values, you need to explore what your highest priorities are.

Living in agreement with their values will make a person feel more empowered, more genuine, and more in control of life. It will help create discipline and help you understand why certain things feel right and others feel wrong. Values can direct someone with career choices. They

can help stir up the strength needed to face a difficult decision. Understanding your values will also help you prioritize matters in your life, set boundaries and expectations, and help make overall better decisions.

Jesus explained the importance of His followers living their lives by His example. In "The Sermon on the Mount" found in Matthew 5, He taught about the importance of how we live our lives.

> *"You are the salt of the earth, but if salt has lost its taste (its strength, its quality), how can its saltiness be restored? It is not good for anything any longer but to be thrown out and trodden underfoot by men. You are the light of the world. A city set on a hill cannot be hidden. Nor do men light a lamp and put it under a peck measure, but on a lampstand, and it gives light to all in the house. Let your light so shine before men that they may see your [z]moral excellence and your praiseworthy, noble, and good deeds and recognize and honor and praise and glorify your Father Who is in heaven." — Matthew 5:13-16*

There are times in all our lives when we make decisions with which we are not happy. Maybe we do something that goes against our better judgment or even against the Word of God. Why do we behave this way? One of the most telling verses about actions in conflict with values can be found in Paul's writing in Romans 7 where he discusses man's succumbing to the temptation to please the flesh even when he knows better.

> *"When one's values do not line up with their actions and decisions, they will feel conflicted, stressed or overall unhappy. It is not unusual for these individuals to begin to blame others for their situation."*

> *"For I fail to practice the good deeds I desire to do, but the evil deeds that I do not desire to do are what I am [ever] doing." — Romans 7:19*

That said, we have to acknowledge that even under the best of circumstances, we are not perfect and we cannot always avoid making mistakes. It is in those times that the grace and mercy of God sustains us and gives us comfort.

The Importance of Values Examined

The concept of values is usually pretty vague to most people. It takes either a particularly insightful individual or one with great discipline to live by their values instinctively. Generally that is because most folks are not aware of the importance of values or what their own values are. It is not until they become conflicted about certain lifestyle issues or beliefs or become stressed by being pulled in too many directions, that they begin looking for a solution.

Take the case of Ashley for instance. She is now 36 years old and cannot figure out why she has not been able to create a more lasting relationship with a man. Born in 1980, she has been surrounded by women friends who live more promiscuous lifestyles than Ashley really feels comfortable with. On one hand she would love to get married, but serious relationships seem to slip from her grasp. She seems to fall into the same relationship patterns as her friends and complains there just are not any good men left. Maybe you know someone like Ashley.

One day someone suggested Ashley speak to a relationship coach. This coach happened to be Christian and Ashley thought they might be a good match since she herself went to church on occasion. When they met, Ashley expressed her frustration about her history of failed relationships. The coach suspected that Ashley might be living with conflicting values. Quite possibly Ashley knew in her heart what would make her happy, but her dreams had remained vague and remote.

Ashley's coach suggested Ashley participate in a values analysis so that both she and her coach would know more about what is really important to Ashley. She and her coach prayed for wisdom and revelation as she began the exercise. By participating in an exercise, much like you will find later in this chapter, they discovered that Ashley's most important values are honesty, faith, helping others, and purity.

Once they compared her values with her lifestyle, it was clear Ashley was living a conflicted life. Her lifestyle had little agreement with what was most important to her. Because she had friends with standards unlike hers, she could not count on them to support her in a Godly way, introduce her to a Christian man with similar values, or even understand her inner conflict. As a result, she felt alone, frustrated, and exhausted by go-nowhere relationships. The coach and Ashley then began to discuss the type of man who would complement the person Ashley deep-down wanted to be. Until now, Ashley was not even aware she was picking the wrong type of man and was instead, blaming herself when things went wrong and break ups occurred.

Soon Ashley became clear about the woman God had created her to be, and realized she needed to proactively seek opportunities to meet like-minded friends. Her coach helped her create a list of ways she could make new friends with similar values and held her accountable to taking the actions needed to bring about these results. This also meant distancing from friends who pulled her into conflict with her values.

Can you see how examining values was a critical, early step for Ashley to begin her process of transformation? Eventually she would become true to God and true to herself. She had to leave some things behind to make room in her life to live in the fullness of God's plan.

Symptoms of Values Conflict

Signs that values may be in conflict include (but are not limited to) when clients:

- Find it extremely difficult to make decisions.
- Frequently second guess themselves.
- Have not set good boundaries in their lives.
- Lack peace.
- Regularly over commit themselves or have trouble saying "no."
- Show or tell of trouble with time management.
- Are putting up with intolerable situations.
- Experience turmoil in relationships.
- Have an inability to set proper boundaries.
- Experience unusual or abnormal stress that sometimes manifests via physiological, stress-related symptoms.

- ○ Find there is never enough time to do what they say is important, yet their lives are busy with matters of less importance.

The above signs are indicators the individual either has not discovered values for their life or there is a disconnect when attempting to apply those values to decisions that they make. When one's values do not line up with their actions and decisions, they will feel conflicted, stressed, or overall unhappy. It is not unusual for these individuals to begin to blame others for their situation.

If you are coaching someone who presents with any or a number of the above, it would be appropriate to recommend one of the values exercises that begin on the following page.

Christian Values

Christian values are drawn from the Ten Commandments and include putting God first, not coveting what belongs to your neighbor, valuing life, telling the truth and so forth. Other values can be found when reading I Corinthians 13, known as the "love chapter." There one can find agape love described.

We usually think of Jesus bringing peace, healing, and comfort, but here is powerful scripture that shows the sovereignty of Jesus and the necessity to uncompromisingly make Him first in our life, above *everything* and everyone.

> *"Do not think that I have come to bring peace upon the earth; I have not come to bring peace, but a sword. ... And a man's foes will be they of his own household.*[A] *He who loves [and* [b]*takes more pleasure in] father or mother more than [in] Me is not worthy of Me; and he who loves [and takes more pleasure in] son or daughter more than [in] Me is not worthy of Me; And he who does not take up his cross and follow Me [*[c]*cleave steadfastly to Me, conforming wholly to My example in living and, if need be, in dying also] is not worthy of Me." — Matthew 10:34 and 36-38*

Values Exercise 1 (Basic)

On a sheet of paper, make a list of 25 or more values you think are important for Christians to embrace. Feel free to use the scriptures for inspiration. To get even more clarity about your own values, complete the following Values Exercise.

Values Exercise 2 (Comprehensive)

On the following pages, you will find an adapted version of the 5-Step Values Exercise I originally designed to be used with the Christian Coach Light© (Leelo-Dianne Bush, 2007) program. Feel free to do this exercise and implement it with others who you believe will benefit from clarifying what is most important to them.

5-Step Values Exercise

(Adapted from Christian Coach Light© 2007)

This exercise will help you clarify your core values, those things most important to you, and then prioritize them to give you added clarity. Please follow the steps outlined below and take your time. Pray for wisdom and discernment as you do this exercise as well as the strength to make decisions that align with your values.

Step 1 – Review the values listed on the next page and feel free to add any you do not see listed. Make sure this list is as complete as possible before you begin.
Step 2 – As you review the list again, circle your 12 most important values.
Step 3 – Now cross off five values of lesser importance, leaving only seven.
Step 4 – Review this list again and cross off four more values, leaving only the top three values on the list.

Write the remaining three values here:

( )_____

( )_____

( )_____

Step 5 – Finally, prioritize the remaining 3 values by adding a 1 for most important, 2 for second most important and 3 for the third most important.

Now you know the top three (3) values in your life. Make sure your decisions, actions, thoughts and words align with these values.

When you line up your actions with your values, you have far less stress, make better decisions, have more confidence, and improved time management. This also demonstrates to you, who you authentically are...the person God made you to be.

VALUES CHOICES

Achievement
Recognition
Ambition
Team Work
Excitement
Determination
Family
Faith
Positive Attitude
Sense of Humor
Financial Security
Material Success
Comfort
Peace and Quiet
Stability
Friends
Family
Honesty
Making a Difference
Helping Others
Leaving a Legacy
Truth
Purity
Respect for self
Alone Time
Power
Love
Joy
Intimate Relationship

Worship
Reading God's Word
Exercise
Passion
Creativity
Self-Expression
Perfection
Success
Excellence
Being Genuine
Wisdom
Fame
Influence
Integrity
Organization & Order
Happiness
Discernment
Hope
Compassion

List Other Values of Your Own

_____
_____
_____
_____
_____
_____
_____
_____

Walking the Talk

Now that you have clarified what is most important to you, it is essential that you take the next step and align your actions with your values. Failure to act in accordance with your values – in a principled way – creates a disservice to yourself and others. When you have clarified what is most important, the challenge then becomes resisting the urge to compromise when work, social pressures, and immediate gratification tempt you to deviate from what is really important. If it occurs, getting off track becomes apparent in any area of life. It often shows up when we make choices that determine how we spend our time. Since most of us have more opportunities and demands on us than we could ever fully satisfy, we need to carefully examine how our values connect with how we invest our time, the one non-renewable resource we have.

Acting in agreement with one's values has even more profound benefits when one is in leadership and able to influence numbers of others. When you act in accordance with your core values (i.e., act in a principled way), you do the "right thing" for its own sake, but you get the added bonus of being a more influential leader. People tend to be more receptive to the persuasive appeals of principled leaders. Leaders who demonstrate integrity have more credibility and engender a higher level of trust. There is less concern that a principled leader will betray others or have a hidden agenda.

As we discover our values and acquire the discipline to live in agreement with them, we begin to see how they will support the passion that drives us to achieve our God-given purpose.

TWELVE

Purposeful Passion & Finding Yours

Your passion is directly connected to your divine, God-given purpose. When we find our passions, we can begin to connect the dots to our purpose. God would not give you a purpose without giving you the desire to fulfill it.

Scripture tells us:

"'For I know the plans I have for you,' declares the LORD, 'plans to prosper you and not to harm you, plans to give you hope and a future.'" — Jeremiah 29:11

Have you ever met someone who tells you they keep having an idea or dream to do something? Perhaps you

know someone with a strong desire to accomplish something that offhand seems impossible. Yet, God has a plan to see it to completion.

> "... when God has a plan and you know it, do not ever give up."

That very thing happened to me at around the age of 30. When I got married, I was very much in love and wanted desperately to have a baby of our own. My husband had been previously married and after two children, opted for surgical birth control. Of course he had no idea that one day that marriage would end and he would later meet me. He could not know that I would have an overwhelming desire to give birth to a child.

I recall researching alternatives and at that time, all medical journals and doctors said his surgery could not be reversed. But I just would not take "no" for an answer. If you have ever known someone who had challenges in this area, you are certainly aware how emotionally charged their life becomes. This went on for several years. Through countless tears, I prayed and prayed for answers. I knew that somehow, someway we would to have our baby. No matter what doctors told me, I just kept on asking and researching. I tell you, when God has a plan and you know it, do not ever give up!

Suddenly one day I ran into a friend who I had not seen since high school. When she learned of my desire, she told me that she was in exactly the same place as I was and she had discovered a specialist in the very city where we lived who had an extremely high success rate with a particular laser technique he discovered. Her husband already had his reversal surgery scheduled.

Well, to make a long story short, God had put everything into place in our lives to make this possible and I did not know it until that very moment. Finances were tight and these surgeries cost many, many thousands of dollars. But God had given me employment with a company, only one of three in the entire country, whose insurance covered this surgery! He even situated me in the same city as the specialist . . . only one of three surgeons who were nationally acclaimed for successful outcomes. My friend became pregnant the same year and my daughter, Ava, was born the following year.

Ava is now an adult and knows how much she is loved and how faith gave her life. I remember all those years, where there was not even one glimmer of hope, yet I believed and consequently my husband believed. We never gave up. God is so awesome!

I told you this story as an example of why you should not ignore your passions and desires. God has a plan but it will only come about if you cooperate. In the Certified Christian Life Coach training offered at PCCCA, there is an in-depth exercise to identify one's passions. You can find it at: http://pccca.org/cplc-cclc

Passion and Passionate People

Some people are just passionate about life. Others have specific passions. Many years ago, some United States military officers commented to me that they had observed my work and found me to be a passionate person. I was a little taken aback until it was explained to me that being a passionate person was far different than being a person who feels romantic passion.

Passionate people are alive with possibilities. They are enthusiastic about anything important to them. They do not just talk about it; they are actively involved with doing something about it. When you talk to genuinely passionate people, their eyes light up when they discuss a topic that inspires them.

It is great to coach a passionate person. When you communicate with them, you just know they understand the process. They want to experience every moment. They are not afraid to take a risk for something they deem important.

A passionate person is courageous. A very wise, elderly woman, whose precise identity I am not privy to, said that, "we must beware of those who lack courage, for in the day of trouble, they will abandon us." Can you think of examples from your own life? On the other hand, a passionate person has the courage of their convictions to remain steadfast in their mission.

Is it possible to lack any passion at all?

Of course it is. I have met a few people who lacked passion; at least when I first met them. They openly admitted that nothing excited them. They also did not seem to possess any special interests. These folks found their work mundane and they were unhappy with their relationships. Those of us who are passionate usually have difficulty understanding how a person could become that way.

Knowing the background and history of these individuals, I can share a few reasons someone might lose their passion. Of the four reasons given below for why someone might lose their passion, most have to do with that person's past.

Someone might lose their passion if:

- The person was browbeaten, discouraged, and cut down as a child, usually by a parent, teacher, or others in a position of authority.
- The person had experienced much difficulty or tragedy to the point they were weary from life and focused only on getting through their day.
- The person had to set aside all personal desires to serve others out of duty, so they stopped dreaming altogether.
- The individual believes lies that they have been told over the years, that they would never amount to anything, so rather than fail, they decided to shut down and not even try. This type of thinking process where there is no use trying anything because it would just fail anyway is called fatalism. "The doctrine that all events are predetermined by fate and are therefore unalterable." (The Free Dictionary) They are afraid of failure or afraid of change, because success would probably bring change.

I find such cases incredibly sad. Imagine going through life with nothing to look forward to, every day being drudgery. Yet some people live that way.

I remember a man I coached in the early years of my practice. He was so duty bound that he had shut down all of his personal desires. He was married to a very strong-willed, professional woman who set all the rules and he had never challenged the way things were. Deep down he knew he was grossly dissatisfied with his life.

> "Keep your eyes locked onto your goal, believe that you can be successful, do whatever is necessary, and do not listen to those who tell you it can't be done."
> — Mark Ingram, 2009 Heisman Trophy winner, on passion.

We began talking about discovering things about which he was passionate. As he started to emerge from the shell he had built around him, he was soon almost giddy with anticipation. He became involved with helping others and applied his professional skills to benefit many in his industry. It was an incredibly fulfilling experience to see such wonderful personal growth. His family and friends soon noticed the changes also.

I knew another person who was so care-worn that the idea of possible change frightened them. Life as difficult as it was, had become their safety zone. At first, they even resisted talking about new possibilities. It is wise to remember that just because we observe what to us seems intolerable, does not mean the other person is ready for something different, even it if is better.

The awakening usually begins when someone asks, "What would you do with your life, if you had all the time and money you needed?" If someone asked you that question, would it not be awesome to be able to answer, "Exactly what I am doing presently."

So now it is your turn. What are you passionate about? If you already know, that is great. If not, just consider what you would want to do with your life if time and money were not a consideration. If nothing readily comes to mind, would you be willing to experiment to see what you like?

Make a list of a few ideas that sound like they might be fun or enjoyable. Perhaps include something that has intrigued you in the past. This can be a bit scary for those who have not stopped to consider these options, but the risk factor is really quite low.

If you try something and do not like it, you do not have to do it again. If you try it and like it but do not love it, it might be something you might want to do occasionally to add variety to your life. But, if you do something and absolutely love it, now you have found a passion!

You will find more on this topic in the Christian Life Coach training and certification courses at http://pccca.org/cplc-cclc/

THIRTEEN

Developing Clear Vision & Mission Statements

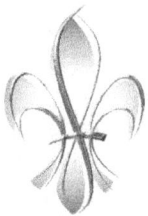

As we begin our study about vision and vision statements, we need to know what God's inspired word says about vision. As we do so, we will learn more about our purpose.

Until I began to really study Proverbs 29:18, all I knew was that unless God's people had a vision, they would perish. That made sense to me in the context of the Israelites. They wandered around for 40 years in the desert because they did not get where they were supposed to go and why. Most of them never entered the Promised

Land. So we can conclude that if we do not know what we are supposed to do and why, we are not going to reach our goals. I imagine most of us are in agreement about this.

But as I studied various translations of this verse, the scripture came alive in brand new ways. Here is the Amplified Bible translation of this verse . . . and it does not just end with the word, "perish." There is a lot more.

> "*If* we do not know what we are supposed to do and why, we are not going to reach our goals."

"Where there is no vision [no redemptive revelation of God], the people perish; but he who keeps the law [of God, which includes that of man]—blessed (happy, fortunate, and enviable) is he." Proverbs 29:18

In other words, if people cannot or will not see what God has revealed to them, then they behave loosely and lose all direction and boundaries. But the person who honors God's Word and aligns his or her actions to it is blessed.

God has a **grand** vision and purpose for all His people, and that is summarized in the Great Commission. Here Jesus starts by stating his credentials, explaining that God Himself, has given Jesus all authority in heaven and on earth. With this authority, He commissions all believers below.

> "Jesus approached and, breaking the silence, said to them, 'All authority (all power of rule) in heaven and on earth has been given to Me. **Go then and make disciples of all the nations, baptizing them into the name of the Father and of the Son and of the Holy Spirit**, Teaching them to observe everything that I have commanded you, and behold, I am with you all the days (perpetually, uniformly, and on every occasion), to the [very] close and consummation of the age. Amen (so let it be)." — Matthew 28:18-20

In addition, God also has a personal vision for each one of us. God reveals our personal vision to us in His time, rather than ours.

> "For the vision is yet for an appointed time and it hastens to the end [fulfillment]; it will not deceive or disappoint. Though it tarry, wait

[earnestly] *for it, because it will surely come; it will not be behindhand on its appointed day."* — Habakkuk 2:3

Furthermore, God reveals His vision to us when we fellowship with Him. If we are not in relationship with Jesus, then we cannot learn the fullness of our vision. Scripture tells us:

"If we say that we have fellowship with him, and walk in darkness, we lie, and do not have the truth: But if we walk in the light, as he is in the light, we have fellowship one with another, and the blood of Jesus Christ his Son cleanseth us from all sin." — I John 1:6-7

As you can see, there are several variables in receiving the vision God has for us.

- We need to be in regular fellowship and relationship with God through prayer and listening to what He reveals.
- We need to align the manner in which we live, with Jesus' teaching.
- We need to wait on God's timing, for the vision to be revealed.

Some coaching books expect you to create a profound vision statement based on their prescribed formula. What is wrong with this expectation? Perhaps you do not have enough information yet. There is no reason to rush this process. By now each of us can create a general vision statement to propel us forward. It might look something like this:

"My vision is to help as many people as possible live the life God calls them to live."

This vision statement is general both in scope and action, yet fairly specific with outcome. As you learn more about God's plan and purpose for you, you can elaborate with more details.

Even if we do not see our vision clearly, there is no need to worry. Jeremiah 29:11 promises, *"For I know the thoughts and plans that I have for you, says the Lord, thoughts and plans for welfare and peace and not for evil, to give you hope in your final outcome."*

We may not know all the details but we know the One who knows. And He will reveal it to us when He feels we are ready.

The Bible makes it clear that God gave visions to people at a variety of stages in their life. Joseph received his vision early in his life by way of a dream and Abraham received his vision when he was 99. Sometimes we receive a little bit of the vision and as we grow closer to the Lord, more details of the vision become clear. In order to become really clear about God's will for our life, we need to totally surrender our lives to Him.

> "I beseech you therefore, brethren, by the mercies of God, that ye present your bodies a living sacrifice, holy, acceptable unto God, which is your reasonable service. "And be not conformed to this world: but be ye transformed by the renewing of your mind, that ye may prove what is that good, and acceptable, and perfect, will of God." — Romans 12:1-2 (KJV)

There is only one way for us to learn God's perfect will or plan for our life.

> "For what person perceives (knows and understands) what passes through a man's thoughts except the man's own spirit within him? Just so no one discerns (comes to know and comprehend) the thoughts of God except the Spirit of God. Now we have not received the spirit [that belongs to] the world, but the [Holy] Spirit Who is from God, [given to us] that we might realize and comprehend and appreciate the gifts [of divine favor and blessing so freely and lavishly] bestowed on us by God." — I Corinthians 2:11-12

Our personal vision must be bestowed on us by God himself, through His Holy Spirit, in His timing.

I have come to the conclusion, after countless hours of study on the topic of vision, that there are only two possible types of vision for our life.

- The vision God has for us – which will always be perfect
- Any vision we create on our own – unless it is the same as God's vision for us, will be flawed.

> "For My thoughts are not your thoughts, neither are your ways My ways, says the Lord." — Isaiah 55:8

There are no other options. The notion that discovered visions and created visions are equally valid, is not consistent with the Word of God.

Many contemporary coaching books teach about creating vision statements and give criteria for doing so. Some even say that the vision statement has to be scripturally correct. Of course I will agree. But there is far more to it. And that is, our vision *must be* the same as God's vision for us. If it is not, then we may be moving toward a goal, but it will not necessarily lead us to our God-given destiny. Because we do not think like the Lord thinks, our vision must be inspired by the Holy Spirit. One way to know if you are discerning the vision correctly is that it will not contradict scripture. If it does, you will know it is not from God.

What must we do then, so that more of our vision can be revealed to us?

> *"But seek (aim at and strive after) first of all, His kingdom and His righteousness (His way of doing and being right), and then all these things taken together will be given you besides." — Matthew 6:33*

God wants us to be completely committed to Him. He does not want us to seek Him only when earthly endeavors fail or if we run into trouble. He does not want us only when man or man's way of doing things has failed. God wants to be first in our lives. Our priority needs to be achieving Kingdom righteousness and when He sees our motivation is correct, He will begin to add more and more to us.

But if you worry about pleasing man or the secular or new-age coaching world, the fear of their opinions will disable you from going forward. However, if you consistently aim at serving the Lord, He will protect and promote you.

> *"The fear of man brings a snare, but whoever leans on, trusts in, and puts his confidence in the Lord is safe and set on high." — Proverbs 29:25*

If you have been trying to do it on your own and you are not achieving the results you think you should, maybe it is not Satan getting in your way. It could be God himself. When I read the following scripture, it transformed how I thought about everything.

> *"...For God sets Himself against the proud (the insolent, the overbearing, the disdainful, the presumptuous, the boastful)—[and He opposes, frustrates, and defeats them], but gives grace (favor, blessing) to the humble." — I Peter 5:5*

So, if we are trying to do things on our own, if we have wrong motives or our priorities are out of agreement with God's Word, God himself will frustrate or defeat us. I don't know about you but personally, I do not want to be out of God's favor.

Just so we are crystal clear, humble does not mean poor or inadequate. The word "humble" means respectful toward God and man, modest and unpretentious, not boastful, arrogant or haughty.

Along with who we are on the inside and our motives, it is important who we associate with. Proverbs 27:17 says, *"Iron sharpens iron; so a man sharpens the countenance of his friend [to show rage or worthy purpose]."*

Creating Your Own Vision Statement

You need to start from the place where you already have a sense of God's vision for you. If you are drawn to Christian coaching, it means you have at least a general idea of your vision. Even if you do not have the entire picture, you can still write a vision statement. There is no need to let this process intimidate you. Just write your statement based on however much God has revealed to you to date.

When you write your vision statement, it needs to inspire and energize you. It should put into words, your mental picture of what you see in the future. And a **God-given vision will always inspire and energize you** rather than make you feel exhausted or frustrated. If it does, it might be a "man-made" vision and not aligned with God. It is entirely possible to create a vision statement that is in agreement with scripture, yet is out of sync with the personalized vision God has for you.

For example, someone may write that they want to become a pastor on a certain time line, yet that is not God's plan for them. Consequently the vision will lack anointing. It will frustrate and exhaust the person instead of operating under God's grace.

Your ideal vision statement will, by its very nature, give you joy, the excitement of anticipation, and make you feel empowered to achieve it. It will bear fruit. This vision should feel organic and natural for you, not contrived.

Before you begin to write your vision, pray for the Holy Spirit to reveal to you, anything else you need to know. Ask for revelation, wisdom, and knowledge. Then be still and wait. In your stillness, consider the gifts and talents God has given you. Consider the desires of your heart and your passions.

Write Your Vision Statement

Next, fill in the blanks on the framework provided below in order to begin your vision statement:

Within the next (scope of time) _____, I sense the Holy Spirit leading me to (action words) _____ _____ with (who or what) _____ _____. As a result, I feel led to accomplish the following outcome(s):

_____

_____

_____

When you state your outcomes, make sure the words are positive and allow God to stretch you. You see, your vision statement should allow for God-size results. The statement should also stretch you personally and require you to step out in faith. You will notice a gap between your capabilities and the ultimate goal. That will be a gap only God can fill as He supports you on your journey.

Remember, God does not always ask you to do something you feel ready to do. Often, He leads you to do something you feel incapable of doing on your own. That requires you to lean on Him and ultimately give Him the glory when you succeed. God will not ask you to do something just so that you can take all the credit yourself.

Review your vision statement at regular intervals, to make sure it is still accurate and current. If you have outgrown your expectations, or you learn more specifics, update your statement.

What if you run into obstacles or problems?

Scripture promises we will have trials yet we will have the strength to prevail. You will learn more about overcoming obstacles in Chapter 15.

II Corinthians 4:8-10 (KJV) states, *"We are hard-pressed on every side, yet not crushed; we are perplexed, but not in despair; persecuted, but not forsaken; struck down, but not destroyed— always carrying about in the body the dying of the Lord Jesus, that the life of Jesus also may be manifested in our body."*

Yet, there is no greater joy than living in the fullness of what God has designed for us to do. And one day when we give account of what we have done with the gifts and talents God gave us, we are told *". . . 'Well done, good and faithful servant! You have been faithful with a few things; I will put you in charge of many things. Come and share your master's happiness!'"* Matthew 25:21 (KJV)

Mission Statements – Move Your Vision to Action

Now that you have a clearer sense of your vision, it is time to move it to action. The purpose of coaching is to help us focus and then act to bring our vision to fruition.

> *"So also faith, if it does not have works (deeds and actions of obedience to back it up), by itself is destitute of power (inoperative, dead)."* — James 2:17

If we say we believe, yet do not act or speak differently, we are only kidding ourselves and others. It could be said we become hypocrites or phonies if we say one thing yet do another, or fail to do anything at all.

As we consider writing our mission statement, we need to know what a mission statement is. A mission statement lays out what you are going to do to accomplish your vision and how you are going to do it.

Why do we need a mission statement? The mission statement keeps us on track and moving toward our vision. In the case of a personal mission statement, it is our guide to taking the needed actions to reach our goal. It embraces and reinforces our values. Organizationally, a mission statement lets the world know what is of highest importance to the leadership of the organization, how the organization operates and in what manner. Mission statements are designed to get others into agreement that the goals are worthy of their support. Here is an example of a mission statement of XYZ Electric Company:

> *"XYZ Electric Company is committed to providing the highest level of consumer value while remaining competitively priced. We commit to researching new ways of generating power and delivering it to the end user affordably as well as offering green, earth-friendly alternatives."*

This is a mission statement that most employees as well as consumers can get into agreement with because it reinforces shared values such as fair pricing, affordability, and green alternatives.

As a coach, you will need to create a mission statement that explains your goal, your priorities and methods of delivering your services. Here is an example of a Christian Coach's possible mission statement:

> "To move my clients from faith to action
> through effective collaboration that provides
> reinforcement of biblical values while focusing
> on my clients' specific needs. I commit to
> provide additional products and services including
> books, tapes and email access
> to further enhance the client's outcome."

As you develop your mission statement, first consider your vision (moving someone's faith to action), then add who you serve (client) and how you deliver the services (focusing on specific client needs, additional products and services including books, tapes and email access). Your mission statement should be designed with the prospective client in mind. As they read your statement, will there be a natural basis of agreement and noble purpose?

Many prospective clients base their decision on whether to contact a coach for services on whether the coach's mission statement speaks to them.

The mission statement must be one that reinforces who you are genuinely and how you operate. It must also bring a prospective client closer to you based on shared values.

Summary

Your God-given vision is enhanced by your values and passions in the following way: Your values indicate what you prize most highly and your passions are internal motivators that propel you forward. Your mission statement offers the specifics about how you are going to achieve the vision.

FOURTEEN

Dealing with Change

All of us have our own way of dealing with change. Coaching may be looked at as a tool that operates as a catalyst for change to occur. Coaches then, are change agents. Because we are in the business of change, we should look at how we deal with change and how we can best help others who are undergoing change in their lives.

Every person who has had an effective, productive coaching relationship, has experienced some sort of change in their life. And each of them has their own way of dealing with the change. It would be great if everyone embraced positive change and took proactive steps to achieve it. That however is not reality. This section is designed to help us understand change, how many of us cope with it, and what we can do to make the experience richer and more beneficial.

While most people have heard of coaching, they may not know how it works. Usually though, they are aware coaches are involved with change. Change is scary to a lot of people. For example, some time ago I spoke with the head of a denominational organization, who told me that their denomination was older and resistant to change. He was just beginning to study coaching and feared that the pastors of churches who report to him would be unwilling to let him change them and how they do things. He stated they seemed afraid that a coach would try to inflict some type of unwanted change on them. Some even feared that working with a coach would be similar to working with a "shrink."

> "Remember ye not the former things, neither consider the things of old. 19Behold, I will do a new thing;"
> — Isaiah 43:18-19 (KJV)

Nothing could be further from the truth. Coaches do not change people based on personal whims. Any action to change a client undertakes is done voluntarily. Prior to the action, the coach and client discuss pros, cons and possible risks, if any need to be considered. The client is fully aware of what they are doing and why.

Coaching is client-driven and coach-supported. Thus in reality, it is the client who comes up with their desired changes or goals. Then the client and coach partner in determining the needed action steps to achieve the client's goal. The coach is there to support the client and hold them accountable to taking the needed steps. This enables the client to take the actions with more information, confidence, and focus than they could have without coaching.

Reactions to Change

People have differing reactions to change. According to Gary R. Collins, PhD in his book *Christian Coaching, Helping Others Turn Potential Into Reality (2001)*, he laid out some major categories to help us understand the way people deal with change.

- **Those who embrace change:**

  - These are people who are often leaders. They love change. Their adrenaline gets flowing at the thought of something new and different.
  - Christians in this category understand that God is in control so it's all good.

- **Those who tolerate change:**

  - These folks usually dread change, but are aware enough to recognize that change happens. They see it, discuss it, sometimes contemplate the impact on their own life, and then usually settle back into life as they knew it, a little uneasily at first and with the understanding that some things will likely be different.
  - Christians in this group feel like life is out of control. They sometimes wonder where God is.

- **Those who view change from a distance but do not want to get involved:**

  - These people are like the news reporters of the world. They look at change. They analyze the impact of change. They get the opinions of others, and eventually draw their own conclusions. They neither fear nor embrace change. They just watch it happen.
  - Christians who fall into this category are generally big believers in predestination.

- **Those who completely ignore change:**

  - This group is living in their own world. They are usually buried in personal issues, family situations, or other matters with narrowly defined parameters. They will always be surprised that anything happened. Unlike the news reporters in the above group, this group intentionally avoids watching the news.
  - Christians in this group usually ignore major events. They have resolved not to get their hands dirty. So change happens, but it is irrelevant to them and their life.

○ **Those who fight change**

- These are the rebels, the mavericks, the protesters in society. They might be of any age, from any socio-economic demographic, but the one thing they have in common is that they radically oppose change.
- Christians in this group are a highly charged contingent. They believe heartily in taking a stand on issues. They believe in activism. They usually know the Word of God and apply it to daily life. Their interpretation of the Word tells them they must take a stand and that stand is: not to change.

Get Ready for God's Next "New" Thing

"We get comfortable and often attached to life as we know it, even if it is not as good as it could be."

"Remember ye not the former things, neither consider the things of old. Behold, I will do a new thing; now it shall spring forth; shall ye not know it? I will even make a way in the wilderness, and rivers in the desert."
— Isaiah 43:18-19 (KJV)

There is nothing in God's Word that tells us to be attached to the past. We need to be future oriented if we are to see through the changes that are needed to fulfill our divine purpose.

"Therefore, if anyone is in Christ, he is a new creation; the old has gone, the new has come!" — II Corinthians 5:17

As mature believers, we celebrate that we are new creations in Christ — but for those who are new to the faith, hearing life will change can be a scary notion. We get comfortable and often attached to life as we know it, even if it is not as good as it could be. I remember as a young believer, I was afraid of change and what might happen, rather than excited. As a child, I had been taught not to hope for anything good so I would not be disappointed. I can see how change might have negative connotations or even inspire fear. Eventually I relaxed into the changes and growth, but that did not happen overnight. I had to unlearn some things as I grew in my faith.

As Christian coaches, we need to be aware we might coach someone who is more reluctant about change than excited about it.

When coaching is on target though, the coach and client become partners who are working to bring about God's plan in the outcome. The client becomes more confident about change and the future.

Transitions Coaching

There is an entire sector of coaching niches / specialties dedicated to transitions, more specifically ... what people go through when there are major changes in their life.

Within these transition specialties of coaching are more sub-specialties including but not limited to:

- Retirement coaching
- Career coaching
- Parenting coaching
- Newlywed coaching

Each of these types of coaching helps their clients deal with change, embrace the benefits of change, understand the anatomy of change as well as the impact of change, and eventually begin to welcome and triumph through change or transitions. The basis for transitions coaching is always at least in part, helping the client become prepared so that they will not find change scary or intimidating.

> "Any time a person wants to improve an aspect of their life, change is inherent to the process."

Coaching is all about change... change for the better. Any time a person wants to improve any aspect of their life, change is inherent to the process. It is important that you understand your own feelings about change as well as the feelings of your clients. Remember that each of them will be unique.

Natural Changes and Consequential Changes

The goal of coaching is to make change take place — but what if we enter a coaching relationship on the heels of a major change in the client's life. Perhaps they are not dealing very well with the consequences of this change.

If someone is having difficulty with change, we need to acknowledge their feelings as valid. There are times when change happens and there is nothing that can be done about it. Some people are in denial about the changes that occur naturally and others that occur consequentially. A coach can ask questions about what has happened or is happening. A coach can help their client clarify by asking:

- How do you feel about the change?
- What (if anything) should be or could be done about the change?
- If the changes are inevitable, then what are the best ways to cope with them?
- Is it possible to embrace the change and if so, what would that look like?
- Let us list alternatives or options for how we may best respond to the change.
- Rate the options 1 to 5 (5 as best) based on viability.

Below is a partial list of life events that create natural changes. These events also cause consequential changes that you need to be aware of. You may be able to list additional changes and add them to this list.

Life Events (including, but not limited to)

- Birth of child/grandchild
- Weddings
- Graduations
- Divorce

- ○ Empty nest
- ○ Death
- ○ Job transfer
- ○ Return to workforce
- ○ Loss of job
- ○ Retirement

And others

Consequential changes may be emotional, logistical, perhaps health-related or financial, etc.

Christian Response to Change

As believers, we deal with change from a different paradigm than the rest of the world. Thus, as we contemplate change and how we will respond, there are some important questions a coach can ask:

- ○ Do you believe this change has been designed by God?
- ○ Do you believe the scripture (Romans 8:28) where it says all things work for good to those who love God and are called according to His purpose?
- ○ Is the change one that enables God's will to be done or is it only an interruption of my personal agenda?
- ○ What is the purpose of the change?
- ○ Beyond the change itself, what are other implications?
- ○ How might they affect the final outcome?
- ○ What are steps that can be executed to make the most or best of the change?

 *Conversation with a Master Christian Life Coach*

Todd Miller, MCLC

As a business and executive coach, Todd, give us your definition of coaching.

In a nutshell, coaching is about execution. It's about taking action. Consider school, for example. When you teach a subject, it is about sharing knowledge and helping someone absorb as much knowledge as possible with the primary objective being to pass the test. Coaching on the other hand, is about action. A sports coach is focused on you taking what you have learned about the sport and applying it to the game on Friday night.

Life coaching is the same way. It's about taking what you know and putting it to use in life. It's about playing the game, not just studying it.

What seems to keep people from taking action in their lives?

To give my best "lawyer" answer, it depends. I hate to say it, but it's true. Every person who comes into a situation has a different past, a different present, and a different future, so they will all have different things that are keeping them from moving forward or taking action. That is just another benefit to coaching. Since coaching can deal with people on a one-to-one basis, the coach can help identify where the person is and specifically what is preventing them from taking the actions that they desire. Then the coach and coachee can address these things head-on.

Have you seen any common themes in the challenges that prevent people from taking action?

Doubt. Doubt, which by definition is the opposite of faith, is probably the number one issue. People doubt their abilities. They doubt their vision. They doubt God. The other, which is doubt's cousin, is fear. People are scared and that fear can be of almost anything. People are scared of failure. People are scared of looking foolish. People are scared of loss. People are scared of success. People are scared of heights and long words. People are scared of all sorts of things, and those fears can be quite crippling.

How do you help people move past their doubts and fears?

There is a verse in II Timothy that is quite useful. 'For God did not give us a spirit of fear or timidity but of power, love, and self-control.' A lot of times we forget this. We think that fear is a natural state of mind because many studies show that we have a natural "fight or flight" response, so we automatically assume those are our only choices. A coach can really help a coachee by reframing their doubts and fears and helping the person see things form a different perspective. We have come to believe that perception is reality, and that's just not true. Sometimes, it is the coach's job to help the coachee see the truth in a given situation versus just their perception of the truth. This is where Christian Coaching is at its best because we have the Word and Truth as given to us in the Bible. Through reading and prayer, we are able to help our clients move forward when others just hit a brick wall.

What are the keys to execution or taking action?

Execution is all about a healthy dose of planning mixed with improvisation. First, poor planning tends to fall into two categories. The first is a lack of adequate planning. Inadequate planning can be anything from a completely non-existent plan to a plan that does not address possible scenarios. It might also be a plan that has inadequate risk mitigation. The second type of poor planning involves too much planning. I have seen plans that are so detailed that people cannot and/or will not execute them. The big issue with these types of plans is that the plan itself has become the end goal. The plan isn't about execution but rather about the plan.

The flip side of the coin is improvisation. No plan will go 100% as expected. You may develop multiple contingency plans based on an extensive amount of risk mitigation, but Murphy's Law says that what will go wrong is the thing you didn't plan for. That's where you have to improvise and adapt to the situation. As a chess coach, I see this scenario a lot in young players. I coach at my son's middle school and young chess players will devise a plan and then stick to it no matter what. The issue with this is that once I figure out what their plan is, I can make almost any move I want and still win.

These two things contribute to the key ingredient in execution – preparedness. A plan is you sitting down and preparing for execution. Then as you begin to execute, the plan provides a certain level of preparedness. However, when you hit a snag, it's time to improvise, and this requires a different kind of preparedness that you get from experience, knowledge and learning.

When I think if execution, I think of the Proverb that says, "The heart of man plans his way, but the Lord establishes his steps." You must make adequate plans, and then trust in God to help you through those times that call for improvisation.

Todd Miller is a Master Christian Life Coach and Coach Trainer with PCCCA, Professional Christian Coaching and Counseling Academy. His coaching practice provides consulting, training, and coaching services to corporations as well as vision and execution coaching to individuals. Connect with Todd at <http://toddscottmiller.com>.

FIFTEEN

Overcoming Obstacles

One of the most important jobs we have in coaching is helping our clients overcome obstacles. Those new to coaching, think this happens by being smarter and more experienced so they can give the client the answers they need. With some experience, coaches find that quite the opposite is true.

The best coaches ask powerful questions. It is important to ask open-ended questions to help clients assess alternatives and come up with their own solutions. As a Christian life coach, if an answer is not in line with God's Word, you should re-direct the person you are coaching to applicable

scripture. Then reconsider their answer in light of the particular scripture reference.

When a person arrives at their own way of solving a problem or overcoming a challenge, they own the answer. They have a greater interest in seeing it through because it fits them. The best questions coaches can ask are open ended. They are questions that the client could not answer in one or two words. These answers would include further explanation.

> ..."*I don't know,*" *is not a productive answer. Ask them to think the question through again and come up with something more substantive.*

When I take this track with clients, they sometimes answer me with "I don't know." I then tell them "I don't know," is not a productive answer and I ask them to think the question through again and come up with something more substantive. This creates a more informative dialogue and makes it possible to come up with more creative solutions.

Agreement to Take Action

Good coaches get their clients moving forward. How do they do this? In several ways:

- They do not allow too much time for discussion about the past.
- They focus on the desired results.
- They challenge their clients to think of ways to get the desired results.
- They hold their clients accountable. Sometimes it is enough for the client to have the perception that since the coach knows of their planned action, they must act. Other times the coach reminds the client that they will be asked about their action and results.

Sometimes though, if we listen closely, we get the impression a client does not have much motivation for taking the action. As their coach, we should ask the client about their level of commitment to taking the agreed upon action. I generally use a scale of 1 to 10. I may ask, "On a scale of 1 to 10, what would you say is your level of commitment to taking this action?" If your suspicions are correct, the answer to this question should tell you whether the client is likely to take the action or not.

> *"You might not be able to change the wind, but you can adjust the sails."*
> (author unknown)

We cannot presume though, that there is only one reason for the lack of enthusiasm to act. This might actually be an indicator that the client has a hidden fear. Maybe they feel the action is too large a step. Maybe they do not understand all of the details. Perhaps they do not see why the action is important. There are a number of reasons. But the bottom line is the client might not be able to move forward unless we discover what is holding them back. This will require us to ask deeper questions.

More about Obstacles

Obstacles can be internal or external. There are some obstacles over which we have control and some we do not. We can change something we control. But sometimes the obstacle is external and we may or may not have control over it.

"You might not be able to change the wind, but you can adjust the sails." (author unknown)

While it is true we often cannot control circumstances, we can control our attitude, our behaviors, and actions as well as the choices we make. That is where coaching comes in. We help our clients make the best choices possible. And the best choices always agree with the Word of God. We should not sacrifice long-term or even eternal benefits for short-term solutions. If the solution is correct, it will stand the test of time.

Here is a partial list of obstacles one might encounter:

- Fear of failure
- Fear of success
- Fear of change
- Worry about others' opinions
- Unforgiveness
- Lack of discipline
- Stress
- Guilt
- Wrong thinking (believing false or irrational statements)
- Lack of finances
- Insecurities
- Waiting until everything is "perfect"
- Fear of taking a risk
- Self-sabotage
- Laziness
- Commitment phobia
- Lack of mentor or role model
- Worry whether they really heard God correctly

And others

Often when the problem is our own, it is difficult to look for solutions objectively. Sometimes we are overwhelmed by our personal thoughts, opinions, "stuff" or baggage, or self-talk. It helps to partner with another individual to process through options so clarity can be gained and the best solution found. Coaching creates a partnership between two individuals who are committed to a beneficial outcome. Thus, options and strategies can be reviewed and choices made with objectivity and scriptural support. Can you see how a coaching relationship can help someone overcome challenges?

Weakness

The Word of God makes it plain that we cannot achieve all God has for us to do on our own. We sometimes cannot even do seemingly simple things without God, such as breaking certain habits. But God designed us so we would have to ultimately acknowledge the fact in and of ourselves, we are not able, but through Him, we are more than conquerors. Our inabilities and insufficiencies are not a surprise to God. He made us so He knew exactly what we would be like. So be encouraged when you don't feel capable.

> "Brothers, think of what you were when you were called. Not many of you were wise by human standards; not many were influential; not many were of noble birth. But God chose the foolish things of the world to shame the wise; God chose the weak things of the world to shame the strong. He chose the lowly things of this world and the despised things–and the things that are not–to nullify the things that are, so that no one may boast before him." — I Corinthians 1:26-29 (NIV)

> "Of this same [man's experiences] I will boast, but of myself (personally) I will not boast, except as regards my infirmities (my weaknesses)." — II Corinthians 12:5

> "And he said unto me, My grace is sufficient for thee: for my strength is made perfect in weakness. Most gladly therefore will I rather glory in my infirmities, that the power of Christ may rest upon me. Therefore I take pleasure in infirmities, in reproaches, in necessities, in persecutions, in distresses for Christ's sake: for when I am weak, then am I strong." — II Corinthians 12:9-10 (KJV)

The Good Kind of Obstacle

Can obstacles be good? I believe they can. Here is how:

- Obstacles can provide learning experiences.
- Obstacles build character.
- Obstacles are opportunities for us to stretch and grow.
- Obstacles make us stronger.
- Overcoming obstacles in our life, gives us testimonies!

I believe God wants us to overcome circumstances in our life with His help so we can experience and then share God's goodness, mercy, grace, and power. God provides us with a way out or a solution so that we give Him the glory.

When I look back at various events and situations in my life I have had to overcome, I thank God for the experiences. Mind you,

I would not want to repeat most of them, but I am grateful for the experience, because now God can use me in new ways. Were it not for the obstacle, I would have had no understanding beyond my shallow observation. Overcoming obstacles qualifies you and me for promotion.

The following scriptures give us confidence as we seek to overcome obstacles:

> "See, the LORD your God has given you the land. Go up and take possession of it as the LORD, the God of your fathers, told you. Do not be afraid; do not be discouraged." — Deuteronomy 1:21 (NIV)

> "A man's heart deviseth his way; but the LORD directeth his steps." — Proverbs 16:9 (KJV)

> "We walk by faith, not by sight." — II Corinthians 5:7 (KJV)

> "Ye are of God, little children, and have overcome them: because greater is he that is in you, than he that is in the world." — 1 John 4:4 (KJV)

> "I can do all things through Christ which strengtheneth me." — Philippians 4:13 (KJV)

> "Come to me, all you who are weary and burdened, and I will give you rest." — Matthew 11:28 (NIV)

> "I have given you authority to trample on snakes and scorpions and to overcome all the power of the enemy; nothing will harm you.' — Luke 10:19 (NIV)

> "There is therefore now no condemnation to them which are in Christ Jesus, who walk not after the flesh, but after the Spirit." — Romans 8:1 (KJV)

> "So too the [Holy] Spirit comes to our aid and bears us up in our weakness; for we do not know what prayer to offer nor how to offer it worthily as we ought, but the Spirit Himself goes to meet our supplication and pleads in our behalf with unspeakable yearnings and groanings too deep for utterance. And He Who searches the hearts of men knows what is in the mind of the [Holy] Spirit [what His intent is], because the Spirit intercedes and pleads [before God] in behalf of the saints according to and in harmony with God's will. We are assured and know that [God being a partner in their labor] all things work together and are [fitting into a plan] for good to and for those who love God and are called according to [His] design and purpose." — Romans 8:26-28

"Who shall separate us from the love of Christ? Shall trouble or hardship or persecution or famine or nakedness or danger or sword? .... No, in all these things we are more than conquerors through him who loved us." — Romans 8:35.37 (NIV)

The Grace To Overcome

What is grace? Simply put, it is the power of God that is available to us, to meet our needs and is a free gift from God. We receive grace through our faith or by believing. When we face a difficulty, we can go boldly before God's throne, asking for God's grace to see us through. Then we need to receive it.

Many earnest believers have found themselves in a rut so to speak, because they have asked for grace and strength, yet have not believed they would receive it. They keep returning to the altar asking for what they need, then doubting that God will deliver or confessing with their mouth that nothing will change.

Perhaps you have a coaching client who needs to know this or maybe this is speaking to you. Each of us have to make up our mind whether we *really* believe God's Word. Do we really want His help? Or do we secretly believe God's promises are for everyone but us? I am asking you these questions, because this applied to me until I learned that my faith to believe for solutions and help, had direct correlation to what I received. If I found myself short on faith, I prayed, asking for more faith. I encourage you to do the same.

I have found that God will give us as much as we are willing to believe for. Not wanting to limit God, I pray, "I ask for your favor and your grace to see me though, Heavenly Father. Please give me the faith to believe for *all* you have for me, Lord, and I gratefully receive it. Thank you for Your goodness and Your grace. Amen."

"Let us therefore come boldly unto the throne of grace, that we may obtain mercy, and find grace to help in time of need." — Hebrews 4:15 (KJV)

"But by the grace (the unmerited favor and blessing) of God I am what I am, and His grace toward me was not [found to be] for nothing (fruitless and without effect). In fact, I worked harder than all of them [the apostles], though it was not really I, but the grace (the unmerited favor and blessing) of God which was with me." — 1 Corinthians 15:10

No matter what our challenge or obstacle, God's grace will see us through. Nonbelievers cannot make that claim.

Celebration and Rewards

It is important we keep the momentum going. Once our clients are on track with taking steps toward their goals, they need us to reinforce their strategies, support their progress and celebrate their accomplishments.

I think it's a great idea for clients to reward themselves with something special when they accomplish major steps towards a goal or the goal itself. For some this might be a dinner out or a day off. For others it might be a Caribbean cruise. It is all up to the person. Planning for and enjoying the rewards of the accomplishment make the process more fun.

List some ideas for how you might as a Christian Life Coach celebrate your client's progress?

1.

2.

3.

4.

Some coaches offer their own special rewards for their clients' progress. I have heard of coaches who give gift certificates, free or discounted sessions, or even financial rewards. It truly depends on what you know to be a motivator to your client.

I recently heard a presentation where a sales coach knew their client to be money-motivated. The client had been afraid to do sales presentations for fear of negative responses. The coach told of offering their client $50 for each "no" they got to their sales presentation within a designated period of time. The coach successfully demonstrated to their client that receiving a "no" was not as bad as the client feared. In fact each "no" statistically brought them closer to a "yes".

Each client has their own motivators and most will not tell you forthrightly what they are. You will have to listen, discern and discover from what your client says or how they say it, just what will inspire them to take actions including the difficult but necessary ones.

SIXTEEN

Necessary Listening Skills

Admittedly, some of us are better listeners than others. But good listening skills can be learned. Every Christian life coach should possess excellent listening skills. Why is this?

We must be good listeners if we are to understand what our client tells us. We need to understand so we can see the whole picture as they see it. We need to see as much as possible of this picture so we can listen "between the lines," hear subtle cues, understand how the client feels without them expressing it, and become an extension of the client. We need to be able to process what we hear so we can ask the right questions.

We need to understand the client so we can see the relevance of God's Word to their situation. Then through the Holy Spirit we can gain more clarity and share this with the client.

The Bible's Directive about Listening

These verses teach us compassion in our listening.

"...let everyone be quick to hear, slow to speak and slow to anger."[16] — James 1:19

"He who gives an answer before he hears, it is folly and shame to him."[16] — Proverbs 18:13

"The mind of the prudent acquires knowledge, and the ear of the wise seeks knowledge."[16] — Proverbs 18:15

I Corinthians 12:25-26 tells us *"That there should be no division in the body, but that the members should have the same care for one another. And if one member suffers, all the members suffer with it; if one member is honored, all the members rejoice with it."*[16]

If we hear things that make us uncomfortable, the Bible tells us to "cast all our cares on Him for He cares" for us. That means we are to share these things prayerfully with God. It is His job to rescue them, not yours. We are to cast the care, and NOT RETRIEVE IT AGAIN.

Philippians 4:6-7 tells us to be anxious for nothing but in everything by prayer and supplication with thanksgiving, let your request be made known to God. And the peace of God, which transcends all understanding, will guard your hearts and minds in Christ Jesus. Any heaviness you feel will be replaced with peace when we leave it with the Lord.

Become a Discerning Listener

Each born-again believer has an ability to discern whether something aligns with the Word of God or opposes it. To increase your ability to discern what you are hearing, seek greater intimacy with the Father.

Use your ability to discern what you hear and don't stifle this instinct. If you sense that something isn't right, pray for wisdom, revelation and greater discernment.

If you are one who has been blessed with an extraordinary gift of discernment, you will find it gives you a special insight in coaching conversations to respond and pray for breakthrough in any situation.

You can read more about the gift of discernment and other gifts that are imparted to us from the Holy Spirit in 1 Corinthians 7-11.

There are those (both Christians and secularists) who feel that coaching precludes trying to figure out what inklings of intuition mean. Spirit-Led© coaching embraces the Words from God, messages, inklings, etc., knowing full well that if we are given a message for someone, it is our obligation to deliver it without filter. That means we present it just as it came to us without explanation. When this is authentic, the recipient of the message knows what it is about, what it means to them and what they need to do.

Without getting too deeply immersed into various interpretations, our goal here is to look for conversational milestones that inspire our curiosity.

- You might sense discomfort with change or transition.
- The client may become unusually quiet or passionate about a topic.
- You may discern a component of fear about the future.
- Your client may seem to contradict themselves or make what seems to be an illogical statement.
- You might see patterns of behavior surface that lead to undesired results.

This is the time to ask open-ended questions that will give you more information. As the client answers the questions, he or she will begin to process their original statement and gain greater insight. This can lead to solutions or answers that were previously not clear or possible.

BARRIERS TO EFFECTIVE LISTENING

TALKING TOO MUCH

Good communication skills are an asset, however talking more than necessary is a barrier to effective coaching. Your client may hesitate to interact with a coach who talks excessively without listening to them. They may either get bored or view the excessive talking as aggression.

The solution is to think before you speak and don't speak if you lack anything important to contribute. This takes self-control. A coaching session is the time for your client to speak and you to listen. Avoid interrupting and be aware of useless small talk that does little more than eat up your client's session minutes.

AVOID MAKING ASSUMPTIONS

Some coaches think they know what the client is going to say before they say it. They then jump in to fill in the blanks or interrupt in some other way.

The solution is to listen until the client stops speaking. We need to listen with an open mind.

ELIMINATE BIAS/PREJUDICE

This happens when the coach lets their perception of their client's appearance or opinions block them from really hearing and understanding fully what is being said.

A close relative to bias is prejudice. This can be described as a preconceived, irrational opinion or feeling. It's very dangerous to the coach-client relationship and has the potential to derail a coaching session. A prejudiced person will not make any effort to listen and understand.

The solution is to focus on the client's words, not on your own thoughts or emotions. Your job is to respect the client for his or her knowledge, experience and skills regardless of the person's background.

ABATE CONTROL ISSUES

In these cases, the coach feels a need to interrupt, hurry, or correct what their client is saying or feeling. Sometimes it may result in admonishing the client.

The solution is to remember we must all meet our salvation with fear and trembling. When it is our time to go before the Lord, we do so alone as does our client. We are not there to FIX anything to our liking. This is between the client and the Lord.

Coaching works because it is a partnership and based on a relationship where one person does not control the other. Coaches are to collaborate with their client as partners, brainstorm, strategize, provide support and love to our client. Remain relaxed and take as much time as you need.

VALUES & BELIEFS

Presumably you have screened each client you work with to ensure that both of you are comfortable with each other's world view, values and beliefs. That said, everyone has their own personal beliefs and it may feel quite natural to want to apply yours to others but we can't do this in coaching. No two people look at everything in the same way.

The solution is to appreciate that others don't have to share your exact beliefs. Often I find that others' unique perspectives help me to learn about issues and answers that were previously foreign to me.

> *"Only when the situation is fully known, can a course of action be considered and intelligent alternatives created."*

If however, you find that your values differ greatly from the client's and you cannot in good conscience keep working with them, it is best to handle this sooner rather than later. Pray and ask God for wisdom about how to proceed. It may be that the client feels the same way. In a conversation, you may want to tell the client that you don't feel comfortable about the direction of the coaching sessions and it may be wise for the client to seek a different coach.

COACH'S EGO

This is where the coach puts his or her needs before that of the client. Each story or situation becomes about the coach, rather than about the client. When the client tells something important, the coach may one-up the client or share something from their own experience that supersedes what the client said.

The solution is for the coach to work at respecting and valuing the client. The coach needs to stop interjecting their own stories. Rather the coach should help the client dissect their story or situation so that a full understanding may be reached. Only when the client's situation is fully known, can a course of action be considered and intelligent alternatives created.

AVOID DISTRACTIONS

Sometimes we can get distracted because we think faster than our client is speaking, or we have seen and solved similar situations before so we think we already know what's coming next.

The solution is to stay in the moment and hang on to each word the client says. Refrain from planning what you will say as soon as the client stops talking. I find it helpful to close my eyes sometimes, so that I can better envision what my client is saying and experience their thoughts and emotions without distractions.

When we truly focus on the client's words, we will get little nudges (and sometimes big nudges) from the Holy Spirit to respond in a certain way or with certain words. Always follow those prompts.

Let me share an example of the Holy Spirit's nudges or unction.

A few years ago, I was in a session with a client, who I knew had a great call on her life, but she was held back by a major obstacle. It seemed like session after session, we kept going back to a poor, pity me posture on the part of the client.

That day, something rose up inside of me that said this had to stop. I knew words were going to come out of me that might shake up the client. I had a little internal "uh-oh." But knowing how these nudges work, I am faithful to deliver a message when I feel the Holy Spirit wants me to say something.

On this occasion I did not know if the client was going to get angry, hang up on me, rebuke my words or... well, I just did not know. I paused, took a deep breath and said, "I feel the Holy Spirit wants me to say something to you here and I hope you receive it in the way it is intended. And the words are: 'When are you going to stop feeling sorry for yourself and start doing the work the Lord has called you to do?'"

My client stopped mid-sentence... there was a very long pause. I just waited. She then came back softly with, "but what happened to me was so unfair ..."

> "*G*od's Word instructs us to be gentle as doves, yet wise as serpents."

I took another deep breath and went on with the strength only the Holy Spirit could inspire at a moment like that: "Do you think it was fair for Jesus to be nailed to the cross and die? He did that so that you and I could be saved. My friend, there are souls out there who need to be saved and until and unless you stop your pity parties, they will be lost. This is life and death, so what's it going to be?" There was silence and I waited.

A moment later, I heard a quiet sobbing from the other end of the phone. Thank God, I thought, I got through to her. Rather, I will say the Spirit got through to her. Thank God too, that she did not hang up on me!

As life coaches we want to make a positive difference in the lives of our clients. We want them to feel good. We want them to thrive, have their spirit renewed, and to find their passion, their calling, pursue their vision, and make their mission come to life. We want peace and joy for our clients. We want to always be pleasant and say nice things.

But sometimes, as much as we want to pass by something difficult, we have no choice but to address it head on and say something tough — to acknowledge things for what they are and to speak the truth as the Holy Spirit leads us. We need to be gentle as doves, yet wise as serpents. Sometimes we are called on to step out in faith that the words the Holy Spirit gives us will be sufficient.

Always act out of love. Always be kind. But listen to those nudges and trust God that as the duty to speak is yours; the results are up to God. Leave the results up to Him.

Looking back, I will admit that even if my client had hung up on me, she would have remembered that conversation for the rest of her life and one day, she would have had to make a choice to change. Fortunately, this was the life-transforming moment for my client. She had carried the pain from childhood neglect with her for the better part of her 30 years. Now she had been set free. Hallelujah!

As Christian life coaches, we must be obedient to our calling. We must respect the will and timing of the Lord for the lives of our clients. Yet, we need to remember that the responsibility for how each client lives their life and makes their decisions is between them and the Lord. To help me maintain the proper perspective in all of this, I have a small sign on the wall of my office that says, **"Duty is mine; the results are God's."** Amen.

Remember that good listening is active, not passive. But what is active listening? When someone tells us something, we give them feedback or paraphrase what they told us. Here is an example:

Client: My boss does a lot of things that undermine my job so it's really difficult to work there.

Coach's response: If I understand correctly, you are concerned that your boss does not respect your work. Please tell me more.

Listening is part of the burden bearing process described in Galatians 6:2. How can we bear another's burdens if we do not learn what they tell us? How can we learn if we don't listen?

SPECIAL SKILLS TO BUILD UPON

It is important for Christian Life Coaches to seek excellence in all they do; in their personal and professional life. It is important for coaches to always:

- Follow the leading of the Holy Spirit.
- Keep the session focused on the client.
- Ask questions that get to the heart of the client's situation and desires.
- Bear in mind you are the Lord's ambassador.
- Keep your clients' matters in confidence.
- Treat your clients with love.
- Respect and honor differences.
- Help your clients envision the future and gain more clarity.
- Resist the urge to give advice or take over the conversation.
- Stay aware of your own values as they help the client gain greater awareness and focus on their own.
- Stay focused on the present and future, not the past.

Listening profoundly is essential when you are coaching someone. Kathy Bateman, MCLC, discusses special considerations when coaching those in major life transition.

 *Conversation with a Master Christian Life Coach*

Kathy Bateman, MCLC

Since you coach women who are going through life transitions such as a divorce or divorce recovery, what is the biggest need you see among women who come to you for coaching?

It is dealing with the loss of the dream – the plan they had to spend the rest of their life with their mate. For many women going through divorce, it is their first opportunity to be heard and set goals as an individual. Prior to divorce, the focus may have been on the couple or on one partner's goals, many times at the expense of the other partner.

After divorce, a woman needs to set her own course, to re-discover her own values, and to plan her life according to the dreams and desires God has placed in her own heart.

A Christian coach can be an excellent partner in offering encouragement, inspiring the client to think differently, and holding the client accountable as they set new goals for themselves as a single person.

What is the first step in helping women transition from the mindset of being part of a couple, to being single?

There could be many first steps, depending on what stage of transition the client is experiencing at the time. While coaching is not counseling, there are some steps that a woman can take to deal with her emotions, while becoming "unstuck" and moving forward with her life.

One of those steps is journaling. I have highly recommended this in divorce recovery classes. While coaching is not about "grief recovery," per se, journaling can be a great outlet for the emotions of someone who is going through a life transition that perhaps they didn't choose, such as divorce.

When coaching, we are working with people who are emotionally healthy, but if someone is stuck in healing or experiencing a state of depression, they should be referred to an experienced professional counselor.

As a Christian coach, I would encourage the client to write the journal entries in the form of prayers or "letters to God." In a crisis or life transition, a person can have one of two responses – they can either turn away from God or turn to God.

I believe it is very important that as a Christian coach, we turn the client to God, reminding them that God still has a plan for their life, even though they are in the midst of a major life transition. I remind the client of Jeremiah 29:11, which says, "I know the plans I have for you, declares the Lord, plans to prosper you and not to harm you, plans to give you hope and a future."

I encourage the client that God still loves them and wants to restore their joy and their hope, no matter the circumstances surrounding their divorce. I have written an eBook, entitled, "Divorce Is Not the Unforgivable Sin," because I want clients to know and experience the grace of God. I believe part of moving forward and becoming unstuck is having the right view of God and how He views us as His children. Once we have the right view of God, we can have faith in His power to redeem and restore.

So I think a big part of helping the client transition through any major change is to help them see the goodness of God, no matter the circumstances with which they are faced.

What are some other ways a coach can make transitions easier?

We have to remind the client that life is a series of changes. There is an old saying that states, "The only thing constant is change." However, it is important to keep some constants, so that we won't be overwhelmed by the changes or transitions we are experiencing at the time.

For example, when I went through divorce, I had to make a cross country move at the same time, and experienced my life being turned upside down, in every way imaginable. The other part of the promise in Jeremiah 29 is where it goes on to say in verses 12-14, "Then you will call upon me and come and pray to me, and I will listen to you. You will seek me and find me when you seek me with all your heart. I will be found by you, declares the Lord, and will bring you back...to the place from which I carried you into exile." In God's great mercy and grace, after a year and a half of living like "a fish out of water," God provided a way for me to come back to the state I had to leave, and I reside here today, in my former neighborhood. I had lost all constants, and it was very overwhelming. So I am indeed sensitive to this area of keeping some constants, having lived the other side of that equation in the worst way.

Developing a sense of community and "maintaining" community is vital. We need to reach out to others and keep in contact with friends and family. This can be especially difficult in a divorce situation because many other people don't know how to respond to those going through divorce. So since they don't know "how" to respond, some don't respond at all! Many times, "we" have to take the step to put others at ease, even though "we" may be the ones who are hurting. And that can be tough for a divorced person or someone going through another type of transition to do, but community is vitally important. A coach can certainly be helpful in encouraging the client to reach out to others while going through a life transition.

Closure is an important step, saying what needs to be said to another, even if we have to write it in a letter that we never send. The coach can encourage the client to take steps towards closure to one phase of life before moving on to the next phase.

Once a woman of divorce has closure, how do you help her to move forward?

Part of moving forward is moving from an attitude of fear to an attitude of faith – and faith takes action! So I try to help the client learn to think and see things differently.

One of the biggest struggles for single women, and especially single mothers, is life balance. They see life as a treadmill with an endless "to-do" list. They lose hope that life can be different, that it can be manageable, and that they really can live an abundant life!

So we want to try to find out what the client is passionate about, what they really value in life, and try to order their life around those values. We also want to get a sense of the Lord's leading in the life of the client. We want to encourage them to act according to His will and His timing.

Once we find out what the client values, we can encourage them to set goals in these areas, starting with the change or changes that will make the biggest difference in their life right now. What changes would make life more manageable as a single mother or single person? What changes will give their life purpose and meaning? What changes can they make so they are living and working in a manner *that is more conducive to their new lifestyle? Can they work from home? Start their own business? Further their education?*

As a coach, we can encourage the client to set action steps towards the goal and help keep them accountable to those steps. The changes the client needs to make may not always be "big" changes. Many times "little" changes can make a "big" difference in the life of someone going through transition. It is important for the coach to be sensitive to the client and to have experience in the coaching niche they have chosen. Many times that experience can offer clues as to what a particular client might need in the way of "solutions." And while coaching is not "advice-giving," a coach can help guide the client at times, if his or her experience has afforded insight into the client's particular situation. Still, the client drives the coaching process and is responsible for setting their own goals and action steps, and is responsible for acting accordingly.

How do you know when you have successfully coached someone through a life transition, such as divorce?

You know that progress is being made when they are moving forward. They are no longer stuck in their emotions. They are setting goals and consistently taking action steps to achieve their goals. The coach should listen with their heart and be sensitive, intuitive, and perceptive when it comes to the client's mood, tone, attitude, and word choice. There will not be negative self-talk on the part of the client, but a shift in both words and accompanying actions.

Kathy Bateman is a Master Christian Life Coach and is experienced in coaching divorced women and single moms through life transitions with a focus on life balance.

SEVENTEEN

Anatomy of Coaching Sessions

You will see that the practical outlines of coaching sessions provided in this chapter will be helpful to understanding how coaching sessions work in a general sense. If you like the initial session anatomy I provide, feel free to use it. However, I do **not** recommend that coaches stringently adhere to the subsequent session anatomy I have offered in this book. To do so would make you a very predictable coach and your sessions might lack a Spirit-led flow, freedom and anointing.

Once you get comfortable with allowing the Holy Spirit to lead your sessions, you will follow a logical sequence and your sessions will naturally F-L-O-W. In fact, if you dismiss what you feel the Holy Spirit leading you to say or do, you can actually get out of the session anointing. So if you are led to deliver a "word" do so. Leave the results to God. You will find two session plans or anatomies on upcoming pages.

Anatomy A – Initial Session

Anatomy B – Subsequent Sessions

ANATOMY A – INITIAL SESSION

1. Greeting, introduction, prayer for wisdom and Holy Spirit guidance in session.

2. Establish overall objective of coaching relationship, based on client forms. For a great place to start, ask, "What one thing, if improved, would make the greatest difference in your life? Then wait for the client to answer fully. You might ask the client, "Would you please tell me more?"

3. Review starting point and circumstances – ask for in-depth clarification.

4. Establish desired outcome or goal(s) – these can be general or specific and should include reasonable timeline.

5. Ask questions to help client outline steps needed to achieve goal.

Dissect first step

What is required from client?

Is there action or "buy-in" needed from others?

Time required

Resources required

Dedication or commitment needed

Other _____

6. Ask for client to evaluate his/her commitment to action. If client is not specific or seems reluctant, ask for level of client's commitment on a scale of 1 to 10, 10 being greatest. Any answer 9 or below, ask client what would raise their commitment to a 9 or 10.

7. Discern any obstacles and ask the client for options to overcome them. You may ask permission to share your own ideas, but get client's input first.

8. Ask client when and how they will know when the goal has been achieved.

9. Ask client how you (the coach) will be able to measure progress.

10. Review next coaching session date, time, place (method) before closing in prayer.

ANATOMY B – SUBSEQUENT SESSIONS

1. Greeting and prayer for wisdom and Holy Spirit guidance in session.

2. Review the desired outcome and specific agreed upon step(s) client was to take by this session. Here the client can discuss what happened since your last meeting.

3. If the client completed the actions he or she committed to, then move on to explore and dissect the next step in the process. (skip #4 and #5 and move on to #6).

4. If the client failed to complete the action(s), ask why. Then proceed to a. or b. below, then c.

    a. If action(s) seemed too large or overwhelming, then dissect the step further and agree upon smaller steps.
    b. If time, resources, or other reason, ask client for 2-3 alternatives or other ways to accomplish the action. Then ask client for yet one more alternative (stretches the client).
    c. Revise this step to manageable size or portion.

5. Re-state desired outcome or goal(s) along with ***revised step from #4*** above continue to step to #7.

6. Ask client to define the NEXT step needed to achieve goal.

Dissect next step

What is required from client?

Is there action or "buy-in" needed from others?

Time required

Resources required

Ask for a BIGGER game – if step(s) seem too easy, ask client for more steps or upsize the step.

Example: Your client is an insurance sales person with a particular income goal in mind. He knows it will take 20 daily cold calls to land four appointments per day to make two sales. On average, each sale brings him $200 commission. The client's goal is to move from $400 daily sales commission to $600. Based on this information you know he needs to make 30 cold calls to increase his appointments and resulting sales, leading to increased income. Ask him how many more calls he is willing to make to achieve higher results. Get commitment to action.

7. Ask for client commitment to action. If client is not specific or seems reluctant, ask for level of client's commitment on a scale of 1 to 10, 10 being greatest. Any answer less than 9 ask client what factors would raise their commitment to 9 or 10.

8. Discern any obstacles and ask the client for strategies to overcome them. You may ask permission to share your own ideas but get client's input first.

9. Ask client how you (the coach) will be able to measure the progress.

10. Review next coaching session date, time, place (method) before closing in prayer.

EIGHTEEN

Practical Procedures & Operations

Students have often asked me how to do sample coaching sessions so others will hire them. I remind them that this is a business. If you are not making enough income to stay in business, you cannot help anyone — not even yourself.

Novice coaches are usually looking for a coaching session script to use or steps to lead each client. The problem is that a client's answers are not predictable. As soon as the client answers in a way that is outside of the anticipated dialogue, the novice coach gets lost. It is virtually impossible to have a contingency plan for everything a client might say or ask.

However, it is understandable a new coach would want some basics as a starting point. At the same time, it is most important for a prospective Christian life coach to understand that each client is unique with a special calling all of their own, with special skills, gifts, and talents, with unique challenges, and so on.

As a professional, we cannot prescribe the same course of action for every client. Imagine if an attorney or physician would prescribe the same or course of action or remedies for every client or patient. They are professionals so they treat their clients as individuals. Therefore a professional coach handles each person based on their needs, not on a preset formula.

This is why Christian coaching is considered a profession that exists as a business or ministry. Christian life coaches are helping professionals, and those who are in private practice can be very well compensated for assisting their clients to arrive at unique solutions.

For the purposes of simplification, there are two types of interactive coaching we can provide:

- Personalized coaching
- Program-based coaching

Personalized coaching generally works one-to-one with the client or couple. The agenda is generally set by the clients. The sessions are client-driven and coach-supported. The client decides the focus of the sessions and the coach accommodates this. Occasionally this type of coaching requires the coach to keep the client accountable and focused on the previously stated topic or goals. This type of coaching is free flowing and allows for an above average amount of session spontaneity. It is also ideal for the Holy Spirit to work through, since the coach (and hopefully client) honors the leading of the Holy Spirit.

Program-based coaching can be provided to both groups and individuals. If coaching is presented to a group, program-based coaching will be most productive and efficient. The key distinction about this type of coaching is that there is a predictable plan in place. At its optimum, this type of coaching propels the participants forward with the synergy created by the group members. The synergy effect is dramatically reduced when program-based coaching is provided to individuals. It can result in rather dry and mundane sessions unless the coach can bring the program to life.

A benefit of facilitating program-based coaching is affordability when used with groups. A novice or beginner coach might also want to present the program to individuals for a reduced fee since it is program-based and lacks the personalization that one would otherwise expect from working one-to-one with a coach.

"Don't be timid during your sample sessions. Ask the client questions or make coaching requests that truly challenge them."

A great reason to use program-based coaching with groups is to allow larger numbers of participants to affordably experience coaching with you. It often inspires individual participants to seek out the facilitator for personal coaching after the program has ended. This type of coaching should be considered a "practice builder" because it is one of many ways to increase your client census. There are other ways as well.

Sample Sessions that Result in New Clients

It is important for the new coach to understand there is one main reason to participate in sample sessions. And that would not be to make the client feel good or give extraordinary value. While there is nothing wrong with a prospective client enjoying the session and feeling good, the most important reason you do sample sessions is so that a prospective client will hire you. Your goal is to present a professional and confident image and excellent client experience.

It is also critical you know that when someone requests a sample session from you, there is a good likelihood that person is shopping around. The sample session is your opportunity to compete fairly with professional coaches who have years of experience. When a prospective client contacts you from a referral or from marketing you have done, you want to respond to their request immediately. I recall an experience a family member of mine had when he was looking for a coach. He must have contacted a half dozen coaches before one responded to his inquiry. Responding quickly will make you appear most professional.

When you set up the session, there is no reason to explain your systems and coaching methods too thoroughly. Your goal is for the prospective client to experience working with you rather than disqualify you for some irrelevant reason. It is also typical for competitors who are "shopping" you to want your inside track for operations. Yes, this even happens in Christian coaching. So if you find you are getting many how-to and system-related questions, simply tell the person that you don't share your proprietary systems. Instead you focus on client results. After all, isn't achieving results the reason a client would hire you?

Some coaches recommend calling the prospective client rather than waiting for their call as you would with a contracted client. You may wish to email or phone them with a reminder of the call a day prior. An experienced coach will have their assistant make this call. The person who makes the call is in charge of the call and can set the pace. When you actually connect on the sample call, tell your prospective client that you would like to start out with 20 minutes of real coaching. Tell them you will coach them like you would a real client so they know this is a real coaching event and not simulated.

Generally this works well for the prospective client because instead of a call where you are explaining the abstract definition of coaching or selling yourself to them, you are instead giving them actual coaching.

Do not be timid during your sample session. Ask the client questions and make coaching requests that truly challenge them. Ask them for extraordinary action. You want this prospective client to be astounded at the difference coaching makes and the actual experience of helping them arrive at solutions.

Example: If you were coaching them on a relationship matter where they want more closeness with their spouse, ask them to describe their ideal relationship. Remind them that with God, anything is possible as long as it agrees with scripture. God created the marriage relationship so any improvement there is a good thing. Next, you can give the prospective client some homework, which will require the two of you to speak again.

Example: If this was a marriage coaching session, suggest the person tells their spouse daily for the next week that they love and appreciate them. They will then call to review results with you the following week.

Coaching in this way helps you separate the wheat from the chaff. If someone is not actually willing to change, they will reject an assignment where they must take action to create change. This will help you see whether you and the client have rapport and would enjoy working together.

Trust me on the following. There is little worse than a client who has to be dragged to action. If you want them to reach a goal more intensely than they themselves want it, the client is likely not ready for coaching. The client must be at least as committed, and preferably more committed to improvement than their coach.

If during this session you get the impression that you two are not a good match, tell the person you do not believe you are the right coach for them. Then have a couple of other coaches' information handy so you can refer them.

However, the prospective client may be thoroughly delighted with the coaching you delivered. They may be waiting for you to ask for their business.

At this point you will want to have a new client packet prepared. This will contain a welcome letter, forms and client contract. Word of caution: NEVER work with a client without having a signed contract (or agreement). The contract will protect the client as well as you in case something doesn't go as well as expected.

In my Advanced Professional Christian Coaching course, I teach a phenomenal session entitled "Conversations that Convert", which contains in-depth training on holding exploratory sessions that convert to paying clients. To fill your practice, plan on taking that advanced course after your CCLC/CPLC coaching course. You will find it at: http://pccca.org/advanced/.

How to Contract your Client

Let us talk now about signing the client. You have just had a fabulous, exhilarating session. The prospective client will be expecting you to ask for their business. So ask and then be silent until they answer. Sometimes people continue doing sample sessions with a variety of coaches until one coach asks them to decide. I usually say, "I have enjoyed coaching you and would love to be your coach. If you are in agreement, I would like to schedule your intake session." Now, be quiet until they respond.

> "*The* prospective client will be expecting you to ask for their business. So ask and then be silent until they answer."

If the response is yes, then proceed to setting up and scheduling their intake session. The intake session is generally longer than the regular sessions, so that the coach and client can get to know one another, the coachable goals can be identified, and a foundation is laid to develop plans and strategies.

If the answer is no, ask them to explain. "Can you clarify your answer?" Again, let them respond before you speak. This will tell you more about why they think they cannot commit. Then you can address any issue, question, or concern. Just asking one more question for clarity shows them you care about the coaching relationship and have a sincere desire to help them.

If the answer is lack of finances, discuss negotiating your fees or payment plans. If possible, you don't want money to get in the way of someone becoming your client, There are also ways to know prior to the sample session that the prospective client has the capacity to pay your fees and are able to make the decision to hire you independently of anyone else's opinion. I include a question on my session request form asking them to rate 1-5 whether coaching is affordable for them at this time. (5 means completely affordable and 1 means absolutely not affordable.)

An excuse sometimes used to get out of signing with a coach is to say they need to check with a second individual. Before I do a sample session, the prospective client also answers whether they need to get the approval of another individual before signing a coaching contract. Then I know they have the funds and are able to commit if they so choose.

Setting Your Fees

As a professional, you need to charge for your services. Unless you charge on a professional scale no client will take you seriously. Low, low fees are a sure sign of lack of confidence or lack of ability. As a coach, you do not want either of those labels. If you are a certified Christian coach, set your fees at or above the $100 per hour mark. You can always negotiate down. The benefit is, no matter where you eventually agree on the fees, your client will see great value in working with you. The more they value your time, the greater their respect for you and the faster they will make progress. It's truly a win-win! We will address fees again later in this book.

Where to Start

When someone contacts you about coaching, it is best to set up a complimentary session lasting anywhere from 30 to 60 minutes. This will give the coach and client time to see whether there is a good rapport and similar worldview to work from. The primary criterion a client uses when they hire a coach is: do they like the coach and do they believe that this coach can help them. Every other criterion is of secondary importance to these two.

In a professional setting you will want to have a welcome packet for each new client. Within the packet you will find:

- A personalized welcome letter from you
- Information sheet asking about the client and their life
- Coaching agreement (sometimes called a contract)

Once the client agrees to work with you and agrees to the fees, they are given or sent a welcome packet. All forms and the agreement need to be returned to the coach prior to the intake session.

During the first session, the best place to begin when you are coaching someone is to ask them to list the **top three things** they would like to improve or change about their life. I ask them this question on their session request form.

Then, when we have our first meeting, I have the client narrow their list down to the ONE THING that if changed, would make the greatest difference in their life. This tells me about their priorities and the urgency of their coaching need.

Once this priority is established, work to get as much information as possible about that specific matter. Usually your client will come up with some great alternatives as they are speaking about the situation. However the deeper you dig and the more closely you listen, not only to what is said, but also what is left unsaid, the closer you and the client will arrive to the solution.

NINETEEN

Business/Practice Overview

In this section we will review important components to setting up your coaching practice. Because this is a comprehensive book on the topic of Christian coaching, it would not be complete without it.

Here you learn to put business into proper perspective as a Christian coach. I will also give you a 14-Step Practice Set-Up Checklist as well as more business planning and development suggestions.

Putting Business into Perspective

I realize some who read this book will not be interested in starting a business or coaching practice.

That's fine. However if you are in coach training, many of the programs will require you to demonstrate basic business knowledge in order to obtain your certification. Even if this is not for you at this time, I encourage you to stay with me for the next few chapters as this information can only help you down the road.

> "It is high time believers start acting like the heirs to the Kingdom that we are."

It is important for us to learn the practical aspects of running a business. I believe it is possible to be so spiritual that one gets out of balance. When doing business we also need to use common sense, be prudent and maintain integrity in all our dealings.

Some of us are called into an obvious form of ministry such as pastoral work or evangelism, but even more of us are called into what I will refer to as marketplace ministry. Rich Marshall, in his book God at *Work*, describes it this way (Marshall):

> "A new breed of ministers is emerging in the world marketplace. These ministers are passionate about the Kingdom, and are people of integrity and high moral character. They think strategically and creatively about ways to impact the world for the Lord. They are called of God and know it, but not in the traditional sense of preaching, teaching, or even evangelism as we have known it. They serve the Lord, but not in church offices or mission headquarters. They serve Him in the marketplace. Why? Because they are business and professional people, and they know that their work is their ministry." (Marshall)

> "They are called of God to make money – a lot of it. Even though they have been warned that this could greatly harm their holiness, they know that God is leading and blessing them. They are called to be creative and to think strategically about transforming their workplace, their city and their nation. They know that God has called them to live for Christ, as lambs among wolves (see Luke 10:3). They believe that God will use them to do miracles in the marketplace. They know that the call of God is upon them to shepherd those believers not currently attending an organized church." (Marshall)

God has created his people kings (business people) and priests (clergy) (Revelations 1:6). We each have a unique function in a practical sense as well as a special anointing for fulfilling God's purpose. If you feel called to serve the Lord, do not automatically assume that means you are to have a pulpit ministry. If you are a business or professional person, you may be called to a marketplace ministry. It may be here that you have an anointing by God. Jeremiah 29:11 says we have each been created with a purpose, and for some, our purpose is to become business people. Why is this?

> *"If you feel called to serve the Lord, do not automatically assume that means you are to have a pulpit ministry. If you are a business or professional person, you may be called to a marketplace ministry."*

The church was not intended to be a profit-making enterprise. It was created to support us, to teach us, to provide fellowship, and offer benevolence to the community. But how will the church continue to survive without a way to pay for its existence and activities? Now you're getting it. The kings (believers in the business world) or marketplace ministers are designed to earn an income and give to the causes of the church.

So if you are a successful business person and feel called to ministry, do not automatically think God is asking you to drop everything and quit your business. Your place may well be in the world as a marketplace minister or a king.

Furthermore, God has created many of us with purposes that cross over from kingly to priestly. Marshall explains in his book that some of us have a priestly calling with kingly anointing or a kingly calling with priestly anointing. One or the other will usually dominate.

Another interesting facet of this is that there are a lot more of us who are called as kings to minister in the marketplace than in the church. Do you know why this is of increasing importance? I believe it is because today so many families are un-churched yet they must be reached in some way.

If people are not in church, God's Word and promises must meet them where they are. And today, where they are . . . is doing business somewhere. You might think of this as a whole new type of evangelism.

> "Let's set aside any notion that it's not blessed to earn an income from a special talent or gift God has bestowed on us."

Let's set aside any notion that it's not blessed to earn an income from a special talent or gift God has bestowed on us. God has blessed us with talents in part so that we can earn an income. If it feels easy and natural to work in your gifting, it's because it's supposed to. Do you think Christian physicians or accountants feel guilty about charging their clients? None do that I know of. Yet each of them is gifted by God to be doing their work. God blesses us so that we can be a blessing to others.

Likewise Christian coaches and counselors have been created by God to help others, to exhort and lift them up, to lead, teach, and partner with our clients to fulfill their divine purpose. There is no need to apologize for that.

It is high time believers start acting like the heirs to the Kingdom that we are. Our God owns everything and is the ultimate provider of all our resources. We need to stop shrinking back because we're "just" Christians. Our God is not broke. We serve the almighty God, the God our provider, Jehovah Jirah!

Look at it this way. If we have less than we need or barely enough, we cannot help or bless anyone. If we're going broke, we cannot even help ourselves. It is ONLY in our abundance, when we are in the place of MORE THAN ENOUGH, that we can make the impact God designed us for as kings. We can then also support the church, the priests, and give to the community. We can feed the poor and clothe the needy. Anything is possible when we have the funds to implement. But we cannot help the poor if we ARE the poor.

So let's get down to business.

HOW TO SET UP A COACHING PRACTICE

14 STEP COACHING PRACTICE START-UP CHECKLIST

1. Do a personal assessment. Review your business management skills, coaching skills, and marketing skills.

   First list your skills and then add a second list of anything that needs work or improvement:

   SKILLS: _____
   _____
   _____
   _____

   NEEDS IMPROVEMENT: _____
   _____
   _____

2. Write a business plan based on your chosen niche. Include any registrations you need to do with city, county, state, or federal government for tax purposes and/or business occupational licenses. Many states do not require licensing for ministries, but be sure to check what your area requires and follow those directives. Also include your first year's operating budget, mission statement, and your income plan including a market analysis. You can find a sample business plan for Christian coaches and counselors in our bookstore at http://pccca.org/bookstore/

   Summarize your plan:
   _____
   _____
   _____
   _____

3. Write your marketing plan and timeline. Use a separate piece of paper if more space is needed:

4. Set your fees and financial policies. See the Business Questions and Answers chapter for ideas on setting fees. Here you need to determine your coaching packages and how much you will charge. You might also include a sliding scale policy and fee structure for working with lower income individuals. Decide if you will have a pro bono policy and how that will work. My personal rule of thumb is to give back or donate at least 10% of what we receive. Do that if you feel led and watch God's blessings roll in.

Summarize your fees and financial policies here:

5. Attach a copy of your *code of ethics* or use the one contained in this book.

   Notes: _____

6. Consult with other professionals including an attorney and a tax professional so that you can best structure your practice.

   List anything that needs work or improvement:

7. Set up your office. Decide whether you will have a home office (90% or more of you will at first, due to dramatically reducing your overhead). If you do so, check your local zoning (city and/or county) to make sure you comply with local ordinances. You may want to consider office-sharing arrangements or find a co-op office. Some office complexes offer ghost offices, where they maintain office space you may use for a certain number of hours per week for meetings. They may offer phone answering and basic secretarial services as well.

   List anything that needs work or improvement:

8. Handle Administrative Details. This includes creating forms you will need or personalizing forms from templates. Be sure to include a welcome packet with client contract, an operations manual or "business in a book", arrange for equipment including phone and computer with round-the-clock internet access. Set up a system for filing client records, a bookkeeping system, open a bank account, liability insurance (if available), and property insurance for your business if your office is going to be outside your home. If at home, you may want to talk with your homeowner's insurance professional to see whether any additional coverage is needed. For security, establish a separate business address and business email address. Generally a post office address (or one with an actually street address such as provided at some mailing/package stores i.e. UPS stores, may work for you).

List anything that needs work or improvement:

9. Create and design your marketing materials such as brochures and business cards, stationery and envelopes.

List anything that needs work or improvement:

10. Create your website or have it done for you. This includes purchase of domain name, hosting, and building the site. Make this professional and do not cut corners. Your clients are hiring you to help them achieve success, and they will only do so if they think you are successful ahead of them. So here appearances are important.

    RESOURCES: We recommend www.heavenly-hosting.com for your website's domain, hosting, security, email and more. For graphic and web design as well as video and audio editing services, visit: http://simplybeautifulmedia.com

    Make a to-do list below and check off when complete:

    _____
    _____
    _____
    _____
    _____

11. Digital calendar on smart phone / tablet or Microsoft Outlook. These are important time management tools you will need. Do not try to remember everything because it will take up important "brain-space" you will need for working with your clients. Save your mental energy! Schedule appointments and important deadlines and dates on your calendar and set an alert to notify you ahead of time. Remember if you are not coaching and handling administrative details, you need to be marketing.

    List anything that needs your attention:

    _____
    _____
    _____
    _____
    _____
    _____
    _____

12. Hire a mentor coach. You will need someone at first to show you the ropes, keep you on track and accountable as you set up your practice. We recommend doing this for your first year, but if you find it unaffordable, hire a coach for at least your first 3 months. I have a special "Power Hour" mentoring program to get you on the right track in a single session and separate fees will apply. Please contact the academy at admin@pccca.org for availabilities.

    List steps you plan to take as you select your mentor coach:

    _____
    _____
    _____
    _____
    _____
    _____
    _____

13. Please list any additional needs you may have so that you can keep that information in front of you and address these items in a timely manner.

List your concern	Contact or Resource
_____	_____
_____	_____
_____	_____
_____	_____
_____	_____
_____	_____

14. Networking Opportunities. List any meetings, clubs, speaking engagements you can participate in to GET KNOWN.

Then contact them to offer your services. Speak for free if necessary and use those opportunities to build your email / contact list.

Notes: _____
_____
_____
_____
_____

As a professional Christian coach, your clients will expect you to run your business or practice with excellence. I am reminded time and again that clients notice everything, including typos in emails and websites, calls not immediately returned, late arrival for sessions and so forth. We need to become credible role models for our clients and demonstrate that we possess the traits of excellence.

 ***Conversation with a Master Christian Life Coach:***

Debbie Stankovich, MCLC

Please tell the readers how you found your coaching niche.

In my former role as a church administrator, it was my responsibility to help people find their place in the ministry of the church. Increasingly frustrated with standard approaches such as spiritual gifts inventories, time and talent surveys, and ministry fairs, I turned to Christian life coaching as a more productive approach for those who genuinely wished to use their gifts in a calling consistent with God's plan for them.

Later in my coaching career when I began training new coaches, I observed that while most people were clear about their passions, they lacked the business acumen and confidence needed to establish a coaching practice. It became obvious that through the years, God had uniquely equipped me to be the person who could coach others in this regard.

What is the greatest obstacle for new coaches in the establishment of a coaching practice?

Every person I have trained has said something along the lines of, "I know this is what God is calling me to do." Most students will tell you that the call to coaching was crystal clear. What was not as clear was the call to business development that accompanied that call to coaching. Of course, many people never intend to go into private practice, but many, if not most new coaches envision coaching as a financial means of support, and it is for that reason they seek training.

Though most coach training programs offer some business and marketing elements, the focus is on practitioner development. Unless a new coach has a business background, ongoing assistance will be required to set up and sustain a financially and legally sound practice. Having a coach to assist with this aspect of their calling is highly beneficial—particularly when the coach is experienced in business and marketing.

What other issues come up for new coaches?

Sometimes what holds a coach back from growing a practice is the false assumption that it is "wrong" to charge people for doing ministry. And, if they can get past that point, many coaches believe that they should not charge for their services. The reasons are varied:

"I'm not experienced enough."
"I need more training before I feel like I can charge."
"I'm not doing this for the money."
"I just want to help people."

How do you help new coaches work through those assumptions?

The people who come to me are there because they have a need to develop business skills. Sometimes the fear they will not measure up as a business person resulted in the dilution of their grand vision. I ask them to tell-the-story again – the story about how God called them to this place. I find that anytime I can get a client to articulate the vision again, the passion for it is fueled.

Then I challenge the assumptions about inadequacy and bring them face-to-face with the underlying insecurities about establishing a practice. When confronted with a question like, "How will the world be impacted for Christ if you pursue your vision instead of the one

God has in mind?" most people will choose God's plan! And what joy it is to then recall all scripture references where God has promised to equip us with all we need to do His will.

As for the financial concerns, I encourage clients to put their issues in a stewardship framework. In the familiar parable of the talents, the master prepares to leave for a while, and entrusts his talents to three servants. To one, he gives five talents, to a second he gives two talents, and to the third servant he gives one talent. While he is gone, the first and second servants invest the talents entrusted to them and double what the master has left with them. The third servant took another path, opting to hide the talent entrusted to him in the ground to preserve what the master had asked him to care for in his absence.

When the master returned, he was pleased with what the first two servants had done, and praised them for being trustworthy, and in some translations, faithful. Their efforts were rewarded, and they were invited into the joy of their master. The third servant was severely reprimanded for what many of us see as a prudent course of action—after all, he took the risk-free route did he not? And do we not even feel sorry for him when the master says that he had been wicked and lazy? But think about it. If everything we have really belongs to God, then how are you using His resources?

People usually conclude that God has entrusted much to those who will multiply His talents and further His kingdom on earth. A mental transference of ownership is not only freeing, it is accurate.

What advice do you have for new coaches?

The first thing I tell coaches is how important it is to make sure their business is operated in accordance with all local, state, and federal laws. As Christians, we are particularly vulnerable to public scrutiny. There are many folks out there eager to see us stumble and point it out to others when we do. High ethical and legal business practices are part of our witness to the world. Paul admonished the people to "Do all things decently and in good order." We must do no less.

The best way to help a coach succeed is to create a business plan. Though usually viewed as a necessary evil, business planning is a highly valuable investment of time. Most community colleges have a relationship with the Small Business Administration and make mentors available to work with entrepreneurs at no cost.

(Editor's Note: Dr. Bush has excellent business planning guides created specifically for Christian coaches and counselors, which are available immediately by download in our academy's coaching bookstore at http://pccca.org/bookstore/)

My recommendation is to look at your business plan about every six months and update it to include new ideas, information, and basically anything internal or external that can impact your goals. The rapidly changing business environment makes revisiting a business plan essential. Nowhere is this more evident than in marketing. Ten years ago social media networking was just that. Now almost everyone in business has a presence on a social media network.

And the most important point is this: the business is just as important as the coaching. Coaches who refuse to recognize this fact will not succeed. But even the person who detests the business aspect of a coaching practice can find ways to accomplish those very important tasks. In fact, doing so is demanded of one professing to respond to the will of God.

Debbie Stankovich is a Master Christian Life Coach, Certified Church Administrator, and Coach Trainer with PCCCA. Her focus is on helping her clients recover from grief and loss as well as having a business / administrative focus. As a PCCCA Certified Joy Restoration© Coach she heads the Grief Coaching Center (http://griefcoachingcenter.com). The organization offers Dr. Leelo Bush's 7 Step Happiness by Choice Method. Debbie anticipates offering career opportunities for Certified Joy Restoration© coaches who wish to join an existing practice.

Learn more about the Certified Joy Restoration Coach course at http://pccca.org/joy/.

TWENTY

Marketing & Branding

Regardless how good a coach you are, unless you master marketing, your practice will never live up to its potential. It does not matter how capable you are if no one knows about you.

That said, this section includes some little known and cutting-edge marketing tips to help you promote your practice, ministry, or business. When I first started my practice, I spent most of my time marketing as you will too.

Let's begin by reviewing some basics and then progress to more advanced marketing.

What is Marketing?

I have heard it said that "Marketing is what you do so you don't have to sell." Not only do you not have to sell coaching, selling coaching does not work.

> *"Marketing is what you do so you don't have to sell."*

Frankly, I do not know of a single coach who entered this profession because they love to sell. Nearly all coaches though, love to help others. Sales and helping others frequently seem at cross-purposes. In reality, those who do well in sales are authentically helping others arrive at solutions. They are engaged in listening closely to the client's needs. They ask lots of questions to find out just what their customer is looking for and then, if their product fills the need, they educate the customer about the benefits of their product. That, at least is how sales is supposed to work.

When I was in my 20's, I had the opportunity to study and become certified by the world's #1 sales training program in its day at an IBM Training Center. I learned how to sell, how to overcome objections, and do so with class, authenticity, and conviction. But when you market more, you need to sell less — or maybe not sell at all. While sales is about approaching prospective clients and demonstrating to them that they would benefit from your offer, marketing attracts prospective clients to you so they are already pre-sold in a manner of speaking and motivated to desire what you offer.

Marketing includes everything you do to bring attention to your work. It may include some advertising. It may include some public relations work. You will find that speaking engagements are an excellent way to let others know of your expertise. Writing informational (not self-promoting) articles about the application of coaching for local, national, or web-based publications will increase your credibility and get you significant attention.

SPIRIT-LED MARKETING© BASICS

What Is Spirit-Led Marketing©?

Spirit-Led Marketing© identifies itself with the Luke 12:12 business model. *"For the Holy Spirit will teach you in that very hour and moment what [you] ought to say."* Luke 12:12

We believe when you have a calling to become a professional Christian life coach, God already knows *who* needs what you have to offer. AND – He will send you those who need your "flavor" of coaching.

Your part in the grand plan is to be:

1. Obedient to your calling
2. Continue learning every day to remain an excellent coach
3. Understand how and do all you can to increase your visibility so others can find you.

When they find you, the Holy Spirit will acknowledge to them that you are who they need to work with.

PCCCA was built entirely upon SLM© or Spirit-Led Marketing© concepts. We receive phone calls from people almost daily who tell us they "knew" PCCCA was the coaching school they had to attend. We know God works behind the scenes every day, bringing prospective students our way.

If you are walking in line with His will for your life, He will do the same for you. Guaranteed!

We came a very long way quickly by God's grace. He has sustained us since 2003 and all the credit goes to Him for making this possible. It has taken lots of work, long hours, amazing technology, expert assistants, remarkable-dedicated trainers along with stellar support staff. Pray and execute, pray and execute gets it done.

You might ask, "If God can do it all, why do we have to market?" I believe we have to give God something to work with. We need to show our commitment to the process. We also need to demonstrate our faith, in order to receive His grace.

So, in order to harness the power of SLM©, we need to pray for leading about where to market. We also need to pray for God to give us the precise words we need to use in order to reach those God has designed us to work with.

Given that you have learned the proficiencies to become an excellent coach, there are a few other things you must do in order to grow your practice and become successful.

You need to become techno-savvy, or be able to hire someone who is, to do your graphic design, website and handle the technical details, sound, and/or video equipment at speaking engagements, etc. We now handle almost every part of this in-house with the exception of a couple of tech experts.

As a coach, you are in the information business. As such you need to continually create new and better ways to connect with your prospective client.

I recommend that you write articles, eBooks, and traditional books that you can sell as an additional income stream. These free and low-cost products enable prospective clients to get to know you without making a major investment. See: http://pccca.org/slm

What Is Branding?

Branding consists of your business image, name, slogan, packaging, and name recognition. All of these components work together to create credibility for you, bring about an emotional tie with your target market, motivate your client to buy, and enhance your client's loyalty to you.

In order to do this you have to understand the needs and wants of your niche market and prospective clients. You put branding strategies into action when you integrate your unique appearance and message at every point of public contact.

Even in a slow economy with thousands of other coaches competing for clients, your brand will be invaluable to help your clients identify you as their ideal coach. You should spend time developing your brand so that your marketing can make maximum impact.

If your branding is done properly, it will not only motivate your prospective clients to select you over your competitors; it will tell your prospects that you are the only coach who provides a solution to their unique problem.

When Should I Begin to Brand My Business or Practice?

There are two schools of thought in this regard. Some believe it is most important you get your practice or business off the ground as affordably as possible and do not concern yourself with branding until you have sustainable income. This is fine theoretically, but without some forethought, your business might seem amateurish. That is not an opinion you want others to have about your operation.

The other way of looking at it is to begin developing a consistent look and feel to your message and materials from the start. It will reinforce your message and increase your credibility, making it appear that your business has a plan, financial stability, and that you intend to be around for a long time to come.

How Do I Create Branding For My Business or Practice?

Define and describe your business or practice. This includes your vision, mission, and values. By now you should have completed your values exercise. Review how your personal values are integrated into your coaching practice. The values should depict the fundamental belief system that predicts how your business operates. This also includes values held by your clients and staff. You might include values such as respect, accountability, and compassion, etc.

Describe your niche, demographic or target market. You must understand what type of client would most benefit from what you offer. If you don't understand your niche prospects, it will be next to impossible for you to remain relevant and competitive in today's market. Make a list of categories that define this group's characteristics such as occupation, approximate age range, male/female, location, income, education, etc.

The more you study this group, the more you will understand about their buying habits. For example, you might discover that your ideal client is a female in the middle income bracket. Upon further study you may discover that this group buys often but spends small amounts. Thus, you will know to plan for and create a selection of affordably-priced, coaching products and eBooks, which your niche consumer can easily afford.

> *"What can you offer to your niche market that solves their greatest problem, which can be presented or packaged in a unique way, which they simply cannot ignore?"*

Create Your Graphics, Collateral Materials and Slogan. If you are unable to create your own logo, website header, and business marketing collaterals (brochures, business cards, letterhead, etc.), then hire someone to create them for you. Your coaching practice colors, type fonts, and style should remain consistent throughout any of your visual promotions and presentations, whether they are an actual tri-fold brochure or a virtual, online image.

The logo should represent your message and be supported by your slogan or tagline. Each time your prospect is confronted with these visual images you'll continue to build an emotional connection.

What Is Your Service or Product (Value Proposition)?

What can you offer to your niche market that solves their greatest problem that can be presented or packaged in a unique way they simply cannot ignore? What does your business do best? This is the message you lead with. You do not want to confuse your prospects by presenting your service/product in multiple ways.

Example: If you coach prospective adoptive parents, you would want your marketing to remain consistent with your message, appearance, slogan, colors, logo, etc. You may want to lead with your entry level product, which could be an affordable eBook that simplifies the adoption process. So, wherever someone might see your promotion for this eBook, they would see your pink and blue logo of a parent hugging a child and slogan, *"Love is a forever home."* This will connect with your prospect on a visual level and on an emotional level.

Marketing strategies (how you tell others about yourself) may change, but branding (your business persona) should remain the same as long as it makes sense. Branding, by virtue of its definition, calls for consistency. A great example of branding is Campbell's Soup. They have a red and white soup can with a script Campbell's on the label. As soon as you look down the soup aisle at your grocery, you can easily identify the Campbell's soup section. Their consistent branding (appearance, quality and message) has made Campbell's a household name.

Review your service or product. Identify the short-and long-term benefits of your service or product. Why is it so appealing to your niche client? What solutions do you offer? How is it priced? Are you willing to offer any quality assurance or performance guarantees? Do you offer any special perks for being your client? An example might be a once-a-month call-in day where any of your clients may call you with a question or laser coaching for 15 minutes.

Create Your Marketing Plan. When you begin developing your marketing plan and budget, keep in mind that your spending has to make dollars and sense. Once you have begun marketing, make sure that it pays for itself. This means if your campaign costs you $500, you need to make at least $500 for it to be worth continuing.

One of the worst mistakes a new business person makes is advertising everywhere without assessing what is working and what is not. Frequently they have not even allocated funds for marketing and advertising, so this activity can very quickly eat up all the operating capital they have. Do not let this happen to you. Every dollar you spend must replace itself.

Keep testing to find your best marketing mix. You will want to be seen in a number of places rather than just one advertisement. Your goal is to appear to be everywhere, without actually being everywhere. Use an integrated approach that includes; sending press releases to publications on relevant topics, print advertising, website, reciprocal links, free classifieds at various websites, pay per click ads and banner web ads. You may want to consider a "banner ad exchange" program where you and other businesses that appeal to the same market advertise on each other's websites. Just research the web for what is available.

Additionally a great way to get known is by social media.

Social Media & Blogs

Make sure that you include social media in your marketing plan. Four of the top social media websites for organized social networking are:

- Twitter
- Facebook
- LinkedIn
- Google+

Other sites offering unique ways to create even more social engagement are:

- YouTube
- Instagram
- Pinterest
- Snapchat
- Reddit
- Periscope

Blog. Every well-integrated marketing approach includes blogging. The word blog actually comes from the words web and log. A blog is a journal of sorts, where you can enter your thoughts or articles and develop a following. RSS (or Really Simple Syndication) allows blogs to forward your posted messages to followers. If you are new to blogging, visit www.blogger.com, which is part of Google, for a free blog template and hosting. This is a great way to start and eventually you can upgrade.

Increased visibility reinforces your marketing plan and then makes it easier for your niche or target market to remember your brand. When you get your campaign running smoothly, the intent is to make it seem like you are omnipresent.

> *"If you advertise the solutions and benefits you offer, you will draw far more attention than advertising your tool, which is coaching."*

How To Advertise Coaching

For some products and services, major newspaper advertising or print media can be very effective. This however, does not appear to be the case with coaching. I believe the reason is that coaching is a tool used to arrive at a solution, rather than the solution itself.

If you advertise the solutions and benefits you offer, you will draw far more attention than advertising your tool, which is coaching. A great analogy is the lawn service company advertising the particularly sharp blades of their mowers (tools) versus the convenience and beauty of a freshly cut lawn (benefits). Which image would be more appealing to you, the former or latter?

I recommend print advertising (newspapers or other local publications) only when the editor or publisher is willing to publish your articles as well. Then those who read about your work will be more informed of the benefits of the solutions you provide in order to decide whether coaching may be for them.

If you are offering a group program, a great way to promote your group is at www.meetup.com or on your church or city's events page. Often they want some lead time to post your event but it's worth checking out. Also, many Christian radio stations offer a community events page and encourage members of the community to participate even if they aren't paying advertisers.

Meet Up in particular is a highly visited website with the specific purpose of connecting people with events in their local area. Each event listed also shows a description, location, and contact information.

Should You Have A Website?

Absolutely! If you want to be taken seriously, a professionally designed website is a must-have in our technological age. The days are long gone where a business person would have to debate whether or not to have a website.

Having a website benefits you in countless ways. Among those reasons:

- It helps people find you.
- It educates people about what you do and how you do it.
- Your website legitimizes your business/ministry.

These days nearly all legitimate businesses have websites. People count on being able to find you that way. Having a strong web presence is even more important than a phone book listing.

In fact, phone books are being used less and less as online searches have replaced their necessity. What's more, when we search the web, we are no longer confined to our city or community. We can literally have the world at our finger tips.

Make sure that your company, ministry, special projects and events have their own web presence. The results can be astounding.

As an example, I started the annual **Christian Coaching Week** event here in Southwest Florida. The event's new website was created at http://christiancoachingweek.com. In 2016, our first year, there were 183 Christian coaches participating all over the United States plus 16 other countries including Brazil, Switzerland, Nigeria, Canada, Cameroon, South Africa, India, Myanmar, Brunei, Namibia, Cambodia, Australia, Zambia, New Guinea, Ethiopia and United Kingdom.

This event created a huge up-tick in awareness about Christian life coaching with local events and speaking engagements. As a result, many lives were changed. Each successive year is an opportunity to expand on these numbers and reach even more. I invite you to visit the website and request information to join us in the coming year.

Rules for your website

If you have or plan to build a website, here are some items you must do in order to make your site work for you. If you do not plan on doing these things, don't bother having a website because it will be a waste of time and financial resources.

Your website (even if you learn to create it yourself) MUST project a professional image.

Your Website needs to grab and hold the visitor's attention within just a few seconds. Most people allow just 5 seconds to determine whether to keep reading a website or click away. 5 seconds!

> "Your site must be crystal clear that you understand your prospective client, their issues, and their philosophy in hiring a coach."

Your site must be crystal clear that you understand your prospective client, their issues, and their philosophy in hiring a coach. Your ability to offer solutions must be *very clear and specific.*

Since your clients will be buying your solution(s), not coaching per se, you need to come across likeable, approachable, and warm.

Be sure to include an attractive, professionally photographed headshot (image of you from shoulders up). More images are helpful and update them regularly. Don't use photos that are over a couple years old and/or no longer look like you. Your prospective clients are buying your time as an expert, a support person, or strategic partner. They will buy or not buy you based on the feeling your site gives them. The visual elements on your website can attract or repel visitors. Images need to draw in visitors every bit as much as the headlines and text on your pages.

Your homepage must be able to demonstrate in a compelling way that you are an expert and can help them. You should use testimonials that describe specific results, your credentials, and a menu of the type of solutions you offer.

Once someone arrives at your website, make it impossible for your visitor to leave without saying YES to at least one offer even if it is signing up for your newsletter or ordering your white paper. If your visitor does not become motivated to take even one action, then you have lost an opportunity to remain in relationship with them.

Granted, maybe not every visitor will get involved, but it needs to be your goal. Your goal should be to get each visitor's email address so that you can continue to communicate with them via email. This builds a relationship where prospective clients can get to know, like, and trust you. When this happens, you become the top-of-mind expert when they decide to seek answers and solutions.

Here are some suggestions on how to do this:

Call to Action Ideas

(1) Offer a free assessment or quiz on your site. You can use www.assessmentgenerator.com to create the html code for it. They also offer remote hosting for your form.

(2) Offer a free or inexpensive report or eBook. Accept payments through PayPal. You can easily sign up for a free account at www.paypal.com.

(3) Offer a 30-minute exploratory coaching session to see whether you are a good match for a coaching relationship.

(4) Encourage your visitor to email or call you so that even if you don't make a sale, you have their email address on your mailing list.

Finally, make sure your website truly reflects who you are, your personality, your abilities, your opinions. Do not be afraid to make a bold statement. Remember, you'll never stand out if your goal is to fit in. Make sure your site is memorable so your visitors will bookmark it for future reference and visits. Also offer a link where visitors can email an invitation to their friends to visit your site.

TWENTY ONE

Coaching Business Questions & Answers

Below are some frequently asked questions about operating a coaching business along with answers.

Should I consider renting office space and arranging for signage?

You could do that, depending on your niche. But most coaches, even those earning six-figure incomes, work from home. Why pay the overhead if you don't have to? Most coaching is done over the phone anyway, because it's more efficient. It is no longer necessary to hire local office staff. Working with a virtual assistant is more efficient and saves you money. Unless your niche requires it, there really is no reason you would need an outside office. Signage is not usually necessary because coaching is not a drive-to service.

Should I market myself as a "coach"?

While this answer seems obvious, it really is not. If your niche is in an industry or demographic that uses the term "coach" then go ahead. If you have a niche where the term "coach" is not used, then it will benefit you to market the benefits you bring to clients, rather than the process you use.

How much time should I spend on marketing and getting known?

Here is an easy formula. Calculate how many hours per week you plan to work on your coaching practice. Let us say it is 20 hours. Let us also say you already have your first client who you meet with for an hour each week. You may also spend a total of another half hour preparing for your meeting and or debriefing from your meeting. That means you are spending a total of 1.5 hours on or with clients.

20 hours – 1.5 hours = 18.5 hours.

There you have it. You should be spending 18.5 hours on Marketing. Now that does not mean you spend 12 of those thinking about it. Instead you spend 18.5 hours actually doing activities to promote your practice. In other words, you spend all the time you are not working with clients – doing what? Marketing.

As your client list fills up, you will have less time to market but you always should retain the bare minimum of 10% of your time for marketing — even if you have a full practice. That is why you need to have a schedule to follow.

There are many great time management programs available. Some are free or low cost. Microsoft Outlook is an excellent computer program for managing your time, contacts, and email.

You want to fill your pipeline so full of prospective clients that you develop a waiting list for your own practice and are even able to refer clients to other coaches, depending on their areas of expertise.

How Do I Determine My Coaching Fees?

You might wonder what coaching fees have to do with marketing. I believe a lot. The following story is quoted from Harry Beckwith's book *Selling The Invisible*:

A woman was strolling along a street in Paris when she spotted Picasso sketching at a sidewalk café. Not so thrilled that she could not be slightly presumptuous, the woman asked Picasso if he might sketch her, and charge accordingly.

Picasso obliged.

In just minutes, there she was: an original Picasso.

"And what do I owe you?" she asked.
"Five thousand francs," he answered.
"But it only took 3 minutes," she politely reminded him.
"No," Picasso said. "It took me all my life."

MORAL OF THE STORY:

Don't charge by the hour; charge by the years.

I believe we can all learn an important lesson from Picasso.

Do not undervalue the gifts, talents, and experience God has given you *and* the service you provide for your clients by charging too little. A lifetime of experience brought you to where you are now; able to help your clients reach their goals.

Each time I raise my fees, I get more clients. Does that seem counter-intuitive to you? It did to me. That is, until I considered who my clients are and what my clients really want.

A typical coaching client is someone who is already doing okay. This person wants to reach a higher level. They believe that in order to be successful, they need to hire a coach who is even more successful. And no professional certified coach ever became successful charging $25-50 an hour.

In fact, a certified coach who charges under $100 per hour is seldom taken seriously as a professional. Seeing the low fees, it is generally presumed the person either lacks confidence, experience or ability, none of which are flattering perceptions.

The reason is pretty simple and you would find out eventually anyway. It's that coaching is quite intense and most coaches can only coach a maximum of four one-hour sessions per day. Add to that a couple hours of administrative or paperwork to support those four coaching sessions and you already have six hours. That leaves two hours for what? . . .all together now – marketing!

If you were coaching four hours per day, five days a week for $25, you would earn $500 per week. Is that the standard of living you want? Most of those reading this may say that would not go very far. Let us change your fee to $100 per hour. At $100 per hour, doing the exact same amount of work, you will earn $2000 per week.

When you multiply $2000 per week by 50 weeks (take a vacation in the other two weeks left each year) – you earn $100,000 a year.

You've got it. You have now made it to the six-figure mark!

NOTE: You can always coach for donation or pro bono if the Holy Spirit lays on your heart to help a particular person. But when you market your services, do **not** list them under $100 per hour. That way, if you do give away some coaching, the recipient will value your services much more and will be far more likely to take the coaching itself more seriously.

Lulls in Your Practice

When you are working for God, just know that every now and then there will be a lull or quiet time. There will be times when you are very busy, and times when you wonder whether there is anyone out there at all.

This used to cause me worry until I understood it. Then one day either I realized it or the Holy Spirit told me; to enjoy the slow times. I learned that these quiet times are for one of two reasons.

First, they may be a time of rest that we need before a busier time approaches. Second, this may be a time to work on a special project that has been put on the back burner. Quiet times are God's way of making space for rest or special projects.

So just know that God will never leave you nor forsake you. He is there for you ALL the time. He is working behind the scenes for you, whether you see the evidence of it or not.

How do I get more traffic and visitors to my website?

Tip 1 – Website Ranking and Traffic

As I have previously told you, a new coach building his or her practice really needs to have a website. It is still the best way to find clients and you are not geographically limited. Show your skills and display testimonials on your site, and you will have as much opportunity to gain new clients as seasoned professionals. Your main objective, once you have a compelling website, is to drive traffic to it.

The site must be submitted to as many search engines as possible. Make sure to verify that your webmaster will do this for you. Also, on the web there are services that can help you with this.

Make sure all meta keywords and the meta description are in place. Determine words your prospective clients use to find someone to help with their problem and use as many of those as possible.

For better ranking, do a search on Google or other major search engines, using the keywords that others may use in looking for you, such as "coaching" or "your city" and coach or other two or three keywords. See who comes up.

Then click on the top three or four websites. When you see their page, right click on a blank part of their page, scroll down to "View Source" on your menu then click "view source." This will show you the html used by the other website. As you review the html on their page, see what key words are being used. Then you will have a better idea of the keywords that can bring visitors to your site.

Tip 2 – Reciprocal links

Have a page on your website exclusively for links and resources. Do a search with the words: **add your link** and another search for **add your link coaching**. This search will bring up websites willing to have you add your website to create an external link.

Some will allow you to input your information and they will link to you. Many of them require you to put a reciprocal link to them, on your website. The more places you can be found on the web, the better the traffic to your website.

Remember, it's a numbers thing. The more people that visit your site, the more people will contact you about your services.

Customer Service

When you get contacted about your services, be sure to reply right away. It is best if you have an auto responder with your email provider. Otherwise, check your email at least twice daily (a.m. and p.m.) so you can answer any questions and start a dialogue.

How To Get New Clients

- Distribute your brochures every chance you get.
- Publish an email newsletter or e-zine.
- Join business networking groups and your local chamber of commerce.
- Offer to speak at clubs and groups for free or fee. It is a great way to build your contact list and pick up new clients.
- Conduct classes at churches or local community centers.
- Collect testimonials from clients and others that know you.
- Tell absolutely everyone you know about your new practice.
- Create a newsworthy press release about a topic of local interest with a coaching tie-in and email it to all local media (newspapers, TV, radio) assignment editors.
- Volunteer with groups in your community.
- To gain experience, coach anyone who wants to be coached, even if it is for free. This will build up your testimonials and referral base.

- Send your brochure and business card to local professionals so they can refer you to their clients. Great sources are accountants, physicians, and attorneys.
- Call the 10 best connected people you know, ask them to lunch or breakfast, and then tell them about your practice.

If God has given you a marketplace ministry, then He has gifted you with the ability to make money. You need to use your resources to bless those in the ministry, who are not positioned to earn an income from their activities.

I highly recommend my eBook, **Best Ways To Get Clients and Fill Your Private Practice Today** in the PCCCA bookstore. You will find it and other great resources at http://pccca.org/bookstore/.

Remember, your coaching practice is a business. Treat it like one. Businesses exist to make money. If you do not know who you coach or why exactly, you don't have a niche. No niche means you have no identifiable customer base. And no customer base translates to no business.

Consequently no business translates to no income. Without an income we cannot do much. We cannot pay for food, clothes, or housing. We surely cannot bless others nor can we help the poor, because we are the poor. The Word tells us that whatever our hands find to do, to do it heartily as unto the Lord.

In Matthew 25, you can read the entire Parable of the Talents but here is the application to our coaching practice: God has given you gifts and talents so that you can use them for His Kingdom. If you are afraid and hide your God-given abilities by not marketing them, then God is not going to bless you with more clients. In fact, what you have will be taken away and given to the one who is willing to work and increase.

You see, once your eyes have been opened to the fact that God wants to use you and you disregard that, postpone it, or fail to act altogether, you will have to answer to God one day. The Word says every one of us will give account of what we have done. Would you not love to hear, "Well done my good and faithful servant?"

Regardless of one's profession, launching out in private practice takes time. Be patient with the process. When a doctor or lawyer opens their office, it does not fill up immediately. They too must let others know that they are open for business, obtain referrals, and market, market, market.

In my case, I knew with certainty that God wanted me to build a coaching practice and develop a Bible-based coach training program. I made up my mind that I was going to build, develop, and market either until it succeeded or the Lord took me home. I really think that's the type of commitment God wants to see in us.

TWENTY TWO

The Uncompromised Truth about Niches

One of the scariest decisions a new coach makes is what their niche or specialty will be. Here are some of the concerns that might go through our mind, explaining why this decision can be full of trepidation.

- If I select a niche, no one else will want me to coach them.
- If I pick a niche, I am cutting myself off from countless prospective clients.
- If I pick the wrong niche, I will be unhappy forever . . . and worse, poor!
- If I select a niche to work in, I will get bored because there is so much else I am capable of doing.

- If I pick a niche, it will limit me. And I want to help a lot of people, not just a few.
- I have no idea what my niche should be, so I will do everything and see what sticks.
- There are not enough people in a niche for me to earn a living off coaching them.
- The thought of saying "no" to clients feels very wrong. I came to coaching to make people feel good.
- I am embarrassed to admit I really do not know what a niche is.

Does one (or more) of these reasons sound like you? Well, rest assured you are not alone. Most new coaches and even some experienced coaches struggle with selecting a niche.

First, let us begin with our operational definition of "niche" in terms of your coaching practice.

A niche is an underserved, specific group of prospective clients who have a *burning* desire for the solution you offer, who are also able and willing to pay you well for such solutions. An optimized niche is actually a specialty combined with an identifiable target market.

What a niche is not:

- A niche is not just a group of people with whom I want to work.
- A niche is not a gimmick.
- A niche should include what prospective clients need, but more importantly it is marketed by offering what they WANT.

A great way to niche is to select members of one specific profession. Why? Because you can more easily identify them and they can identify each other in order to refer you as someone who specializes in their industry and solutions they need.

Let us take a look at criteria to help you select a niche. Remember, you can coach anyone you want or feel led to coach, however this is business. Unless you earn an income you are out of business. So this is a practical list of niche criteria.

NICHE CRITERIA

Do you have a passion for working with a particular type of client? It is not enough for your niche to compensate you highly. You should find enduring satisfaction in working with this group.

Does this group have a compelling desire for the solution you offer? The magnitude of their "want" will be proportionate to the level of their interest in purchasing the solution you provide.

Is your proposed niche underserved? It is a lot easier to become the #1 sought out expert in a field where there is not a lot of competition.

Does this niche already exist? If it exists, that removes some of the risk. It shows that this group is able to support the coaches that serve it. If you are entering an existing niche, then take a look at how your competitors are serving this niche. Tailor your approach and provide easier access, better service, or greater value. Learn everything you can about the specialty and this market group so that you will stand out as the expert above the rest.

Can your prospective clients afford to pay for your solutions? And, even more importantly, will they pay? A niche that is comprised of displaced women returning to the work force, for example, is not one that can support you. It is easy to find these women, and though they may need and benefit from coaching, they do not have the resources to purchase your services.

Narrowing your niche may feel counter-intuitive, but if it is difficult for someone to describe what you do and specifically who you serve, odds are you don't have a customer base.

Coach trainers, industry thought-leaders, marketing experts and naturally, successful coaches all agree that choosing a viable coaching niche is your first step to creating a flourishing coaching practice. Success leaves clues and this is one of them.

EXAMPLES:

If you think you have a niche coaching Christian women, that is not nearly narrow enough. Suppose you are interested in coaching Christian women who are parents. That is a start, but each age group of children have unique issues so let us try to refine this even more. Why not narrow it to Christian women who are parents of pre-schoolers? Now you have a niche because they have something in common and they are looking for the same type of solutions.

Suppose your goal is to become a business coach. Business coaching is too broad to be a niche. Even if you add Christian to business coach, it is too broad. You can actually take specializing with business coaching into a number of different directions. How about coaching *small* businesses? I will argue even this is not narrow enough. Let us take it one step further. A true niche would be to coach owners of small businesses who happen to be physical therapists. A viable niche might be physical therapists that own medium to small clinics who need help growing their clinics. This leads to the next criteria.

> "*W*hen you focus your efforts, you can market much more affordably and effectively."

Focus on one profession or industry if possible.

This will allow you to focus your marketing efforts and solutions specifically for this one group. When you focus your efforts, you can market much more affordably and effectively. Look for publications and associations that serve this group. Learn all about the challenges experienced by this industry. Then submit articles to the publications. Others in ancillary businesses who advertise in their publications may be prime candidates for joint venture partnerships.

Are you helping this group in one of the three KEY areas of life? These areas are finances, relationships, or health. If so, your client base will find it much easier to justify paying you for your knowledge, services, or information because the results are of critical importance to them.

Do you personally have experience in this field? If you have been there, done that, and found the solution, it will be much easier for prospective clients to relate to you. Your experiences and solutions will instantly connect.

Is the solution you offer in demand for the short-term or long-term? It just makes sense to offer solutions to a sector that will continue to need them as well as updates over many years to come.

Example of short vs. long-term business solutions:

News reports warned that computers might crash at midnight January 1, 2000 if they were not millennium-compliant. Many computer businesses set up special consulting services where they would check computers to ensure Y2K compliance. When New Year's Day 2000 arrived and nothing noteworthy happened, the programs ended. That was an example of a short-term solution.

A long-term solution would be offering transitions coaching for baby boomers. Statistics show their numbers are steadily increasing and their needs are fairly predictable. Those include retirement lifestyle options, post-retirement second careers, health and wellness concerns, and financial coaching for retirement.

Can you find and reach your niche? Do they live in a particular locale? Do they communicate in a special or unique way? Do they read certain industry publications or blogs? If not, how will you be able to identify them and communicate with them? Or, if you are marketing to develop an email list of prospective clients, how will they find you? How will they be able to recognize or identify that you offer their needed solution?

How to become #1 – Template

"Most coaches make the mistake of offering very general coaching, solving very general problems, for a very wide audience. The problem with this approach is that you're competing with tens of thousands of other coaches," says Milana Leshinsky, a veteran coach and niche advocate for nearly two decades.

"Out of hundreds of coaches and experts I have consulted, collaborated with and interviewed in my... years as a coach, I haven't met a single one," said Milana, "who achieved a *really high level of success* without specializing."

That is true, but you have to understand one, simple, unfailing principle. Not only do you have to specialize, but you have to offer a service or product that your niche **wants** and is willing to pay for. Marketers call this a "hungry market." There is a simple formula to help you in this process. And this formula, once you achieve one success, can be repeated over and over again.

The idea is to provide services and products that address the burning issue of your niche. Nowadays, the number one place people go for answers is the internet. They surf until they find what they need. Sometimes people do not even know they need exactly what you offer until they come upon it. When you have identified this "hungry market," you essentially need to create three offers.

Your first offer will be one that captures the contact information. Once you have this information you will create an email list. An email management system is needed for this purpose. Offer something that gives the "what" answer that the prospect is looking for. But do not give it all away here. Save the "how" for the higher-end product or service you offer. Here is an example:

Let's say you are a website strategy coach. Your clients want to know how they can optimize their website for maximum sales. Your eBook, *How to Maximize Sales from Your Website* answers their question. In it you list everything one must do in order to get the maximum amount of sales. After reading this valuable information, the client may have a follow-up question: "But how do I do these steps?" In response to the "how" question, you have developed the higher-end product or service. This may be coaching personally with you, or better yet, an in-depth product that spells out the step-by-step "how." The reason I prefer the product approach to this, is so that once created, it can be put into the system and your time is not tied directly to your earnings. Otherwise, coaching one-to-one limits how many clients you can work with, how much you can charge, and at what point you reach burnout. Since none of us want to work so hard we burn out, the product is the logical solution. Another reason is that having a product to fill this need frees up your time to create another niche and replicate this system.

With your first or entry product, you have demonstrated you understand what they need. Your second offer is a back-end product that fulfills the need. Then you collect testimonials from satisfied clients and post them on your website. Because your niche has received a very personalized solution from you, they gladly refer you to anyone else who shares this need. They feel good about referring you because your service or product has been so reliable, has arrived quickly, and has solved their problem.

Your third product is a no-brainer. This one provides a level of continuing support. This might be a coaching club or membership website that your clients subscribe to on a monthly basis. This third in a series of products will provide you with continuing (residual, recurring) income. You have already established trust with these clients. This third product will keep more information and support coming from you, their trusted source.

This relationship needs to provide *more than* the perceived dollar value based on what the members receive and yet be reasonably priced so that your members cannot afford to discontinue. As a result, you and your clients will continue in a win-win, lifelong relationship.

Now that you have the template, pray about the niche and direction God would have you take. The key is to discover and develop your niche, one that is unique to you.

 ***Conversation with a Master Christian Life Coach***

Jenny Grace Morris, MCLC

Why do some people feel it's difficult to come up with their niche?

Many times when an individual feels called to become a Christian life coach, they see how natural that is for them. Friends, family, and coworkers have come to them before and have relayed problems or challenges they are facing. No two situations were exactly the same and so the individual wanting to become a coach feels they want to be a generalist in the coaching field. Otherwise they think that people whom they could help will not come to them if they specialize.

Another reason people don't always find their niche is because they don't recognize their natural ability to relate to certain groups of people. They overlook this talent because it comes too easily for them and don't really see it as a niche or even as a need."

Can you give examples of helping someone uncover their niche?

Yes, the most important step though is listening to God first. Then as I listen to students' stories you can hear when they get excited about a topic, group of people, or an area of expertise. One student was passionate about helping unwed mothers but recognized it would be the volunteer side of her coaching practice. She really felt that she wanted to be a generalist because she had vast life experience. This was certainly true. However, it was pointed out to her by me and those close to her that she had approximately 30 years of business experience with a large amount of that time designated to owning one. She was an expert on how to start, maintain, and develop a successful business. It was easy and natural for her to do this and she could become a coach's business coach.

Another woman always told stories about how she helped one man with his troubles or another man with his challenges. It never occurred to her that this was an area in which she was naturally gifted. It sounded too simple and she questioned me about it at first. As she listened for God's guidance she realized this was true and that she had grown up with many brothers. The men she knew were not comfortable going to another man for help but drawn to talking to her.

Suppose someone feels lead to a niche in which their interest is enormous but their actual experience may be limited?

When a student approaches me with this question I first give them an example of someone who was very successful as a coach but not necessarily famous for doing well at what they coached. The example was Lee Strasberg, most noted for being a great acting coach and teacher of Method acting. Did people remember him from the films they saw? Generally the answer is "no." Yet, people had the best coaching growth with him.

One of the students from PCCCA had always wanted to help executives. However, he had not been an executive in any firm. Yet many of his ideas were brilliant because they were founded on Biblical truths. He would give examples of how he thought something should have been handled in a company he worked for and others commented on these suggestions in a positive way. Sometimes this occurred even after the company went in the wrong direction. His passion for executive coaching was apparent and he decided that the only obstacle to saying he was an executive coach was himself.

Are there questions you can ask that will help an individual discover possible niche(s)?

There are many questions a coach can ask or one can ask of themselves if they are self-coaching. Some are:

- *What areas or topics are you passionate about?*
- *What do you do for fun?*
- *What are your hobbies?*
- *If you were going to volunteer anywhere, what would you do and where would be the most rewarding place?*
- *Is there anything in your current employment that you would miss if you were doing something else?*
- *Is there any one thing people consistently compliment you on? Who comes to you for help?*

Then see if there are similarities with the people coming to you.

Suppose someone's niche is teaching coaching to groups. Do they have to be specialized?

Many coaches enjoy public speaking and bringing groups of people together in either a seminar or workshop setting. You still want to be specialized.

There was a student who wanted to give seminars on relationships. I have noticed that most people think in terms of marriage when it comes to relationships. But married or not, we all experience many types of relationships. If that were your niche, you could have unlimited topics for group sessions. This would also be true for other topics such as finances.

Jenny Grace Morris is a Master Christian Life Coach and Trainer with PCCCA, the Professional Christian Coaching and Counseling Academy. Her website is <u>http://jennygracemorris.com</u>.

TWENTY THREE

Ethics, Accountability, & Best Practices

Since coaching, specifically Christian life coaching, is an unregulated profession, it is important for coaches and the industry to manage and govern itself. As Christians, our coaching principles of conduct should be governed by scriptures. Allow me to guide you.

> "As iron sharpens iron, so a friend sharpens a friend." — Proverbs 27:17 (NIV)

In this chapter you will find ethical guidelines, standards for accountability and best practices.

ETHICAL GUIDELINES FOR CHRISTIAN COACHING

Ethics: The rules or standards governing the conduct of a person or the members of a profession (The Free Dictionary).

Below you will find the revised Christian Coach's Creed (also known as Christian Coach's Code of Ethics):

Christian Coach's Creed

(also known as Christian Coach's Code of Ethics)

© Rev. Dr. Leelo-Dianne Bush, 2006, rev. 2007, 2008, 2009

I believe in Jesus Christ, who is my Lord and Savior.

I believe it is my duty to uphold Jesus' teaching as found in the Holy Bible, in my own life and actions, as well as within my relationship with anyone I coach.

I believe that to whom much is given, much is required. As a Christian life coach, my personal life must be completely above reproach. My actions or omissions shall never lead anyone to doubt my faith or their own.

I believe it is my duty as a Christian life coach, to point to the Holy Scriptures as God's inerrant plan when my client is uncertain, confused or at a loss for direction and particularly if my client's direction appears to be aiming away from the truth found in God's Word.

I believe my relationship with my client should be Christ-centered and client-focused, where my goal is to help my client with their God-given purpose and living true to it.

I believe it is my duty to maintain the confidentiality of everyone I coach, unless information is released by the client or such confidentiality conflicts with the prevailing law or court order. Otherwise, information shall remain confidential unless it is deemed that such information could be illegal, harmful or dangerous to person or property.

I will maintain integrity in all business and personal dealings; performing as I commit to perform, referring clients to others if the client's needs do not match my competencies.

I believe my sessions are to be led by the Holy Spirit, and I must be ever ready to speak the truth in love, as I am led.

My goal is and will always be: personal and professional excellence.

I believe that when I am weak, God is strong. With God in it, nothing is impossible! Amen.

_____ /_____

    Signature of Coach   / date

A few years ago, I presented a session at the annual Christian Coaching Conference in Ft Myers, Florida on the topic of ethics and accountability. As Christian professionals, we are to hold each other accountable.

God has set up an orderly way to confront errant behavior. You will find God's perfect plan for conflict resolution and correction in Matthew 18:15–17.

Accountability

First and foremost, we are accountable to God. Working as a coach who considers themselves Christian is vastly different from working as a *Christian* coach. This is not just about semantics. As the latter, we must put God first, personally and professionally. Our work requires that we understand and honor the leading of the Holy Spirit. It is our obligation to become knowledgeable about scripture because we can only uphold God's Word and share its power when we know what it says. God holds us each accountable.

> "So then, each of us will give an account of himself to God." — Romans 14:12 (NIV)

> "And let us consider how we may spur one another on toward love and good deeds." — Hebrews 10:24 (NIV)

Secondly, we must be accountable to one another. Because our profession is not regulated and there is no official oversight, it is important that we hold each other accountable. In the absence of supervision we need to develop relationships with other Christian life coaches who will hold us accountable to maintaining and raising our standards.

> **"B**ecause our profession is not regulated and there is no official oversight, it is important that we hold each other accountable."

In order to develop any relationship with accountability, we must be able to trust the other person. We must feel that our accountability partner is one who will listen to our concerns with a non-judgmental heart.

As Christian coaches, we have similar goals and challenges. This understanding will enhance our bond with one another.

The scriptures below give us specific direction on developing accountability and how to treat one another. These verses make accountability so clear, that I see no need to expand further on them.

> "BRETHREN, IF any person is overtaken in misconduct or sin of any sort, you who are spiritual [who are responsive to and controlled by the Spirit] should set him right and restore and reinstate him, without any sense of superiority and with all gentleness, keeping an attentive eye on yourself, lest you should be tempted also. Bear (endure, carry) one another's burdens and [a]troublesome moral faults, and in this way fulfill and observe perfectly the law of Christ (the Messiah) and complete [b]what is lacking [in your obedience to it]." — Galatians 6:1-2

"Therefore encourage one another and build each other up, just as in fact you are doing. Now we ask you, brothers, to respect those who work hard among you, who are over you in the Lord and who admonish you. Hold them in the highest regard in love because of their work. Live in peace with each other. And we urge you, brothers, warn those who are idle, encourage the timid, help the weak, be patient with everyone. Make sure that nobody pays back wrong for wrong, but always try to be kind to each other and to everyone else." — I Thessalonians 5:11-15 (NIV)

Accountability Questions:

- Do you have an accountability partner?
- Will that person hold you accountable professionally and personally?
- Are you the kind of person who has strong boundaries and high ethical standards, and who has the ability to hold another person accountable?
- Why or why not?
- As a coach, do you hold your clients accountable to their spiritual walk?
- Do you hold those you coach accountable to doing what they commit to do?

If you do not have an accountability partner, list some steps that you can take to develop that kind of relationship:

_____
_____
_____
_____
_____

Best Practices

Definition of Best Practice(s) – Methods and techniques that have consistently shown results superior than those achieved with other means, and which are used as benchmarks to strive for. There is, however, no practice that is best for everyone or in every situation, and no best practice remains best for very long as people keep on finding better ways of doing things. (Business Dictionary)

As with any profession, over time we have developed a list of best practices for Christian coaches. However it should be noted that since coaching relationships depend on a great deal of interaction and personalization, there are but a few best practices that nearly all coaches will agree can be used successfully in every situation. Among Christian coaches, the list is distinct and largely unchanging.

Christian coaches distinguish themselves first and foremost as followers of Jesus Christ. Because scripture tells us that God remains immutable, our coaching practices remain the same from yesterday to today and tomorrow, even to the end of time. Why? Because God's Word delivers its intended outcome every time. God is no respecter of persons, that he should change the rules for one over another. God does not show favoritism nor should we.

> *"For God shows no partiality [undue favor or unfairness; with Him one man is not different from another]." — Romans 2:11*

> *"...Peter opened his mouth and said: Most certainly and thoroughly I now perceive and understand that God shows no partiality and is no respecter of persons, But in every nation he who venerates and has a reverential fear for God, treating Him with worshipful obedience and living uprightly, is acceptable to Him and [a]sure of being received and welcomed [by Him]." — Acts 10:34-35*

Therefore, sound practices for Christian coaches generally remain fairly constant and unchanging. Here are some generally accepted best practices for Christian coaches:

Highlight and emphasize the importance and power of prayer. You may choose to begin and end sessions with prayer. Also reinforce the client's need for personal prayer time as it is the single best way for one to one communication with God to occur.

Treat those you coach with love and do not judge them. That does not mean that we approve of sin or that we coach someone to sin. Let that never be the case. Rather, we need to be aware of and gently point to scripture as the guide.

Honor the leadership and guidance of the Holy Spirit. Share same with client to the extent you deem it appropriate in the setting or needed within sessions.

Let us always keep the confidence of our client, unless such confidence would conflict with prevailing law or unless this information received in confidence might endanger person or property.

Do not tell your client what to do. If you have something to offer in a session, in addition to what the client has arrived at, ask if you may have the client's permission to share your thoughts or suggestions, as the case may be.

Do not coach those who you are not qualified to coach either by experience or training. Have a list of other coaches, counselors or professionals to refer the client to. You will find that the prospective client will appreciate your honesty and respect your decision. Further, should the opportunity arise for them to refer you to others, they will be confident in your integrity and far more likely to tell others about you.

Establish your coaching relationship fees and terms with documentation, forms and a contract (some refer to this document as an "agreement"). It protects both parties legally and will help avoid misunderstandings later on.

Maintain the protocol of having the client phone or visit the coach for their session, as it may apply. In this way, the client makes an effort on his or her own behalf. The more highly a client is invested in the coaching relationship, the more seriously they will take themselves, their actions and their progress.

Maintain professional liability insurance for your practice. Since we live in a litigious society, it is prudent to protect your interests. Your coaching contract limits your liability exposure in many cases. But if you are required to defend your business practices, prudence and ethics, you may need to hire an attorney. That can get very expensive, very quickly with retainers, etc.

If you have been unable to locate this coverage on your own, the Professional Christian Coaching and Counseling Academy offers a resource for affordable, professional liability insurance to our students and graduates.

Perhaps you can come up with a few more best practices of your own.

_____
_____
_____
_____

Research and list other resources to support you with best practices.

_____
_____
_____
_____

TWENTY FOUR

Future of Christian Coaching & Professional Growth

Christian life coaching can benefit nearly everyone, regardless of age or stage in life. Spirit-led, Christian life coaching adds the power of the Holy Spirit to Christian life coaching, making this the most powerful type of life coaching available to the world today.

Since by far a majority of those who receive Christian counseling do so for situational problems and not clinical or mental health issues, adding Spirit-led, Christian coaching techniques and proficiencies will make a counselor far more effective. Your clients will progress much faster since they will take accountability for their own actions. You will help them create and implement strategies in line with God's will and destiny for them.

> *"Spirit-led, Christian coaching techniques and proficiencies will make a counselor far more effective."*

Even those who do not have a Christian Counselor certification can learn the profession at PCCCA and add these new skills to their Spirit-led Christian life coaching practice. Some may use these skills within their church or ministry. Others may want to learn in order to improve their own life or the lives of others around them (See details at http://pccca.org/counseling/).

We encourage you to renew yourself daily by studying the Word of God. Pray for guidance and discernment. Keep growing by studying. Seek excellence. Speak abundance into your life and the lives of others you know. Use your gifts to help others.

HOPEFUL ECONOMIC FORECAST

Surprisingly Good News

During the last decade, we have seen difficult economic times. I have long said eventually the pendulum will have to swing in the other direction. I think we now have reason for great hope that things are improving overall. There is a great resurgence in the jobs market and economic indicators, including the stock market peaked at a 110 year high.

When times are tight financially, the extras, and coaching is often looked at as an extra, are the first things to go. Corporations sell their jet planes and lay off their pilots. And for the rest of us, if it's a choice between paying our mortgage or life coach, the life coach sadly, has to go.

Christian coaches are now in even greater demand than ever before. There are good reasons for this. Christian coaching has now become much better known and respected. Our clients' success has led to a greater number of referrals to Christian coaches. The ease of reaching those who need us has greatly improved with new technological advances and the growth of social media outlets.

> *"Christian coaches are now in even greater demand than ever before."*

If you are considering making Christian coaching your career, think about whether you are willing to do what it takes to operate your own business or whether you prefer to work for someone else. Most Christian coaches (at least those my academy trains) start their own practice or find employment in private industry, government and social service agencies. Some work in non-profits or in conjunction with mental health organizations or clinics, providing coaching to sustain positive behaviors. There are many options.

One of the most attractive features of having your own coaching practice is that you don't have to leave your day job to begin. You can start with very low overhead expenses. Basically all you need is a computer and phone. There is no reason to rent office space. Even most 6-figure coaches work from home. Since there are few if any geographic barriers, you can work as a virtual business. Rather than hiring staff, you can develop a virtual support team.

It is simple to run your business part time in the evening or on weekends. Then transition to full time when your practice will support you.

It takes dedication, persistence and commitment to make it work. I think God tested me for a long time to see whether I had what it takes to stay in this industry, before he blessed us with great growth. Know that it will take time and it won't always be easy. It's supposed to be this way to develop your inner character traits so that you will grow into the best coach possible to serve your clients.

CONTINUING EDUCATION

Your Commitment to Lifelong Learning

I read recently that learning to become a life coach is a marathon rather than a sprint. Should you decide to become a Christian life coach, whether as a vocation or avocation, you must make a commitment to lifelong learning. Your clients will rely on the excellence and your own personal growth that you bring to the coaching relationship. You need to take the journey yourself before you can take your clients to their goals.

Formal and Informal Education

Some ways to continue your education are:

Enroll in a Certified Christian Life Coach training program. If you have already completed this program, pray about participation in an advanced course or the Master Christian Life Coach program. These are offered at the Professional Christian Coaching and Counseling Academy (www.pccca.org). At this time I am not aware of any others that have the same biblical foundation and business training as my proprietary courses.

If you are unable for whatever reason to participate in formal training, I recommend that you begin a reading regimen. Make a commitment to read at least one book per month. You will find some great resources in the academy bookstore at http://pccca.org/bookstore. There is an assortment of useful resources on that page. If you don't find what you are looking for, please contact the academy from the contact page at http://pccca.org/contact/.

Coaching Groups and Masterminds

There are a number of ways to create coaching groups and masterminds. They can be formed by invitation, by public forum, via mailing lists, website promotion, application, social media, etc. There are paid groups and free ones. You will find that generally, members of the paid groups will be more helpful and members will have a higher commitment level than free ones. It just makes sense that members are more engaged and helpful when they have made an investment.

Coaching groups and masterminds are not, I repeat, not networking opportunities. Rather, they are groups where you can get feedback, support, and ideas for your business or practice. Each of the members in this group must be committed to providing and upholding a safe place to support one another. If you are starting the group, make sure that:

- If you have members from the same specialty, they should not be competitors in the same market. The threat of competition will stifle the group as members will be reluctant to share ideas for fear their competitors will exploit them. An example that would work is organization coaches, each of whom lives and promotes in their own city and state.
- If you have members from random specialties, they may be from one city or area as long as they do not compete. These members will be unified by being coaches and sharing similar concerns, but not in direct competition for the same clientele.

Hire a Mentor Coach

If you are a new coach starting out or an experienced coach wanting to take your practice to the next level, hire a coach who is already at the place you would like to be. They can relate to your concerns, while at the same time offer you constructive advice and resources. They can share what worked for them and save you the time it takes to learn from all the same mistakes. For those who want to shorten the learning curve, mentor coaches are a great investment.

I want to work with you if you are ready to dig in, work hard and grow your practice or business into all it can be. I offer virtual and on-location VIP days to help you develop a successful, sustainable coaching practice. It is what I love to do. As a serial entrepreneur, I am never short on creativity and battle-tested tactics to take you to the next level. You are not required to be a student or graduate of PCCCA to participate. Learn more at http://leelobush.com/vip/.

Find Joint Venture Partners

When you are looking for joint venture partners, you will find ideal matches among those who are already serving the same market as you, just in a different capacity. Look for those who have something you may lack. For instance, if you have a special skill but a small or non-existent mailing (email) list, look for those who have a large email list. Any collaboration has to be a win-win situation. When you approach a potential partner, lead with what's in it for them. The first question in their mind will be, "how will this benefit me?" So be prepared to volunteer that in the first 15-30 seconds. Will it bring your prospect greater visibility, more clients and higher sales? Then you will have their attention and the rest may just be about planning your joint project.

Devise a Weekly Plan and Stick to It

Your plan should be prioritized according to Matthew 6:33. Start your day with the Lord. You really can't afford not to. If you say you do not have time, then you need to modify your priorities. If you want God's blessing, He must be in first place. He wants to be involved in every facet of planning.

If you haven't done so already, develop a morning ritual including devotions and prayers for wisdom and guidance. Then be still and wait to hear what God would have you do. If you have asked God for direction but still are not sure what to do, I would like to suggest perhaps you have not listened for His reply. God doesn't usually "shout" to get our attention. He generally speaks gently with few words. So stop what you are doing and listen. Pray, and take time to just be still and listen.

Maybe God will bring something to your remembrance or perhaps a new idea will pop into your head. He communicates with each of us in a way we are able to receive and understand.

If you are a new coach and do not have many clients, then spend your time marketing. If you are an experienced coach, then maybe it's time to delegate some duties that are not directly related to income or those that are administrative in nature. If someone else can do them, they should. Your duties should exist of coaching, developing / creating products, networking and strategic planning.

> *"To one he gave five talents [probably about $5,000], to another two, to another one–to each in proportion to his own personal ability."* — Matthew 15:15

You may recognized the scripture above. It was taken from the Parable of the Talents in Matthew 25. This parable is used widely to demonstrate that God wants us to do all we can with the gifts and talents He gives us. At this time, I would like you to pay special attention to the words above, "to each in proportion to his own personal ability".

We first need to show God that we will make the most of what He has given us. If we either do nothing or hide our resources and talents, God calls us wicked. By the end of this parable, even the one measly talent the servant had was even taken away from him and given to the one who had five. *"And throw the good-for-nothing servant into the outer darkness; there will be weeping and grinding of teeth."* Matthew 25:30

There are several take-aways from this parable.

- Do all you can with the resources you have.
- Don't be lazy.
- Don't be fearful.
- The greater your abilities, the greater your opportunities for increase.

And here is one that we do not talk about nearly enough:

We have the capacity to increase our own abilities. In fact, you and I are the only ones who can do this. How? By learning as much as we can about our profession, by honing our skills through practice and by working diligently to multiply what we have been given.

You see, God has left a lot of this up to you and me. What will we do with what we have been given? Our life experiences are not random. Rather they have been our training ground to create the foundation of God's plan for us. God already knows who needs that special gift or experience we have. It is up to us to execute the steps to make it happen. All of us will have to give account one day.

Life happens to all of us. Each of us has our own variety of challenges, hurdles, discouragement, and setbacks. But God wants to use all of us regardless and He has promised that He will never leave us or forsake us. If you sense an unusual flurry of negative activity around you as you start out, receive this as confirmation you are on the right track and Satan is trying to stop you. The greater the attack, the bigger the destiny that awaits you. By all means don't stop. Remain confident. God plus you are a majority and will prevail in victory at the end!

So take account of your resources. Pray about how God would have you use what you have been given. Then get busy!

My Prayer For You

Dear Heavenly Father,

Please watch over and guide every person who reads this book. Give them open hearts to understand Your Word and open eyes to see the needs in their community.

I ask in Jesus' precious name, that you help each person discover God's unique plan and vision for their life and help them do all they can to achieve it.

Remind my friends to seek first your kingdom and your righteousness and by your loving grace and mercy, remind them that you will provide ALL they need according to your riches when they make you first.

Help them to maintain balance in their life so they don't unknowingly give the enemy an opportunity to hold them back.

Encourage them at times when they feel weak. Let them know that is when you will show yourself strong to carry them through.

Please give them wisdom so they deal wisely with your resources. Show them how to stop the compromise with worldly values and give them the strength to do so.

I pray that one day when they stand before you, you will tell them "Well done, my good and faithful servant."

I pray all this in Jesus' name. Amen.

Bibliography

1. Business Dictionary. (n.d.). Retrieved September 13, 2009, from www.businessdictionary.com/definition/best-practice.html

2. The Truth Project. Focus on the Family. Retrieved from http://www.thetruthproject.org/

3. Gary R. Collins, P. (2001). *The Biblical Basis of Christian Counseling for People Helpers*. Colorado Springs: NavPress.

4. Gary R. Collins, P. (2001). *Christian Coaching: Helping Others Turn Potential into Reality*. Colorado Springs: NavPress.

5. Hilton-Goode, E. (n.d.). Ezine Articles. Retrieved October 22, 2009, from http://ezinearticles.com/?id=59088

6. Jones, L. B. (2004). *Jesus, Life Coach*. Nashville: Thomas Nelson.

7. Marshall, R. *God at Work*. Shippensburg: Destiny.

8. Milligan, P. F. (2006, March 25).

9. Sanders, J. O. (1994). *Spiritual Leadership*. Chicago: Moody Press.

10. *Staff. (n.d.). Peer Resources. Retrieved October 22, 2009, from Peer Resources:* http://www.peer.ca/coachingschools.html.

11. *The Free Dictionary. (n.d.). Retrieved 2009 15, August, from* www.thefreedictionary.com

About The Author

Leelo Bush, PhD is president and founder (2003) of PCCCA, the Professional Christian Coaching & Counseling Academy, which provides exclusively Bible-based, Christ-centered and Spirit-led training programs for Christian coaches, counselors and the public. Program and enrollment information along with testimonials are available on the web at www.pccca.org.

She is also producer and host of the popular *Christian Coaching School Podcast* and its predecessor, the *Reach Higher Show*. Both are available on iTunes and other major podcast outlets.

An entrepreneur, marketing expert and former TV talk show host, Dr. Bush is a Christian coaching thought leader and trainer as well as sought after guest on radio and TV.

A yearly focus for Dr. Bush is the annual Christian Coaching Week, an international event. She created this celebration for Christian coaches around the globe, not only for PCCCA students and graduates. It is their opportunity to share Christian coaching and raise awareness and credibility for our industry. All Christian coaches regardless of their affiliations are invited to participate. You can find more information about this event at http://christiancoachingweek.com.

Most of Dr. Bush's work currently involves administering the academy, training Master Christian Life Coaches, business / marketing coaching, creating curriculum, writing, speaking, and other creative projects.

Dr. Bush and her husband, Evan make their home in Cape Coral, Florida, along with her toy poodle. She has one adult daughter, Ava-Laine.

For more information, training or scheduling,
contact Dr. Bush at:

Leelo Bush, PhD
Professional Christian Coaching & Counseling Academy
c/o Beautiful Life International, LLC
1217 Cape Coral Parkway, #159
Cape Coral, FL 33904

Phone: 239.471.2806 (US)
Email: admin@pccca.org

Courses & Training Programs created by Dr. Bush

CCLC/CPLC (Certified Christian Life Coach / Certified Professional Life Coach) program offered at PCCCA

Advanced Professional Christian Coach Certificate Course

MCLC (Master Christian Life Coach) program offered at PCCCA

Certified Christian Counselor program at PCCCA

Joy Restoration Coach©/Christian Grief Coach certification program offered at PCCCA

Stress Relief Coach© certification program offered at PCCCA

Relationship Communication Specialist certification course Collaboration with Jenny Grace Morris, MCLC

Spirit-Led Marketing© unparalleled business promotion course for Christians

Bestseller Blueprint
How to write and market an Amazon bestselling book.

Dr. Bush's Guide to Product Creation with Workbook bundle

Christian Coach Light© group coaching program

Certified Group Coaching Facilitator course – due out 2017

More program details are available at http://pccca.org or by calling 239.471-2806 (US).

Other books and digital products by Dr. Bush

Business Success Planning Guide
for Coaches & Counselors

Best Ways to Get Clients
Fill Your Private Practice Today

Unlock the Secrets to Divine Increase

Decision Making Guide – Pro Version
Master the art of decision making like highly successful people.

Top 5 Uncomfortable Money Questions and How to Answer Them
Includes Set of Scripts

How to Create a Business Plan
for Christian Coaching / Counseling

Secrets to an Irresistibly Beautiful Life

Leadership Goldmine: 24K Nuggets for Lasting Success
Compilation book with 6 Master Christian Life Coaches

How To Start A Christian Coaching Ministry

How to Start A Christian Coaching Practice

Dr. Bush's credits also include publishing numerous magazines, a newspaper, and authoring periodicals, articles, and newsletters.

Certified graduates are located in nearly every US state and Canadian province, Mexico, South and Central America, Caribbean Island Nations, Europe, Middle East, Asia, Africa, Australia and New Zealand. PCCCA training is available internationally.

For Quantity Orders of This Book

Visit the website at

http://christiancoachhandbook.com

Index

A

abandonment, 70
abilities, 7, 50, 54, 56, 124, 189, 197, 223
ability, 22, 50, 72, 83, 89, 138-139, 161, 187, 194, 197, 206, 213, 223
abnormal, 96
Abraham, 110
absence, 59, 175, 212
abundance, 23, 55-56, 61, 71, 166, 218
abuse, 60
Academy, 6, 14-15, 29, 42, 126, 208, 215, 220
academy, 172, 176, 219-220
acceptable, 48, 82, 110, 214
accomplish, 3-4, 24, 84, 90, 102, 113, 115, 134, 153, 176
accountability, 2, 27, 30, 41, 80, 181, 209, 211-213, 218
accredit, 14

accreditation, 13-15, 51-52
accredited, 14-16, 52-53
accurate, 114, 175
achieving, 4, 23, 26, 89, 111, 158
acting, 149, 166, 206-207
activities, 165, 192, 197
activity, 183, 224
Acts, 59, 63, 83, 214
adapt, 125
adhere, 151
adjust, 129
administrative, 171, 176, 194, 222
admit, 144, 200
admonish, 213
adoption, 183
adrenaline, 119
adult, 103
advanced, 28, 66, 160, 177, 220
advertise, 184-185, 202
advertisers, 185
advice, 2, 26, 46, 48, 71, 145, 149, 175, 221
advocate, 58, 204
affiliations, 13, 16

afford, 182, 201, 205, 222
affordability, 115, 157
affordable, 161, 183, 215
affordably, 115, 157, 181-182, 202
afraid, 12, 49, 79, 81-82,
    103-104, 118, 120,
132, 134, 189, 197
Africa, 186
Agape, 36-37
agape, 36-37, 79, 97
Age, 12, 41
agenda, 31, 67, 90-91, 100,
    123, 156
aggression, 140
Agnostic, 41
agnostics, 41
agreement, 14, 33, 44, 55, 93,
    95, 100, 108, 112, 115-116,
    159-162, 215
alert, 72, 79, 171
align, 23, 80, 98, 100, 109
almighty, 166
Alpha, 92
alternative, 73, 153
alternatives, 23, 102, 115, 122,
    127, 141-142, 153, 162
amateurish, 181
amazed, 71
ambassador, 9
ambassadors, 7, 34-35, 37,
    53, 145
Amen, 108, 133, 144, 211
American, 36
Amplified, 108
analogy, 27, 185
analysis, 95, 167
analyze, 119
anatomies, 152
ANATOMY, 152-153
Anatomy, 151-152
ancillary, 202

anger, 36, 72, 138
angry, 143
anointed, 76, 85, 90
anointing, 76, 112, 151-152, 165
antagonistic, 41
anxious, 138
apologize, 166
apostasy, 13
Apostate, 13
apostate, 13, 46
Apostle, 61
Apostles, 57
apostles, 4, 83, 133
appointed, 14, 108-109
appointments, 154, 171
appreciate, 72, 110, 141, 159, 215
approachable, 187
approval, 17, 161
approve, 4, 69, 214
approximate, 182
approximately, 206
April, 4
argue, 202
arrogant, 10, 37, 112
article, 4, 14, 61
articles, 178, 180, 184-185, 202
articulate, 59, 174
ashamed, 7
Ashley, 95-96
aspirations, 77
aspire, 75
assess, 27, 52, 72, 127
assessment, 167, 188
assessmentgenerator, 188
assignment, 159, 196
assistant, 12, 83, 158, 191
associates, 14, 26
associations, 202
assumption, 174
assurance, 5, 76, 183
assured, 132, 200

Assyria, 79
astounded, 53, 158
atheist, 63
attitude, 129, 148-149
attorney, 156, 169, 215
attorneys, 197
attractive, 187, 219
attribute, 34, 49
audience, 61, 203
authentic, 12-13, 15, 42, 79, 139
authenticity, 53, 178
author, 6, 58, 70, 129
authority, 9, 13, 104, 108, 132
Ava, 103
awakening, 105
awareness, 58, 76, 85, 145, 187

B

background, 15, 104, 140, 174
baggage, 130
balance, 36, 49, 64, 148-149, 164
balanced, 35, 64, 81
baptizing, 108
barriers, 23, 70, 219
baselines, 75
Bateman, 145, 149
battle, 221
battles, 79
beginner, 29, 157
beginning, 22, 92, 118
behavior, 46, 139, 211
behavioral, 52
belief, 40-42, 53, 55, 181
beliefs, 11-12, 41-42, 52-53, 55, 93, 95, 141
believer, 2, 13, 17, 40, 42, 44, 58, 63, 120, 138
believes, 16, 63, 104

believing, 40-41, 59, 130, 133
belongs, 19, 97, 110, 175
benchmarks, 213
beneficial, 83, 117, 130, 174
benefit, 23, 43, 66, 87-88, 98, 105, 124, 157, 161, 178, 181, 192, 201, 222
benefits, 5, 15, 57, 73, 100, 121, 130, 178, 183, 185-186, 192
benevolence, 165
beseech, 110
Beth, 70
bias, 140
Bible, 3, 9, 13, 16, 22, 25, 31, 35-37, 40, 42, 45, 54, 56, 58-63, 108, 110, 125, 138, 198, 210
biblical, 3, 12-13, 23, 42, 56, 58, 75, 79, 115, 220
biblically, 52, 59, 71, 78
big, 56, 70, 119, 125, 142, 147, 149
bigger, 78, 224
biggest, 145, 148
birth, 102, 131
blame, 12, 94, 97
blamed, 28
blaming, 96
bless, 19, 57, 166, 197
blessed, 82, 108, 139, 166, 219
blessing, 31, 67, 78, 83, 110-111, 133, 164, 166, 222
blind, 44
blog, 184-185
blood, 63, 109
boast, 36, 131
boastful, 10, 31, 111-112
bodies, 35, 110
body, 4, 14, 35, 114, 138
bold, 27, 189

boldly, 133
bonus, 100
bookkeeping, 170
books, 35, 43, 109, 111, 115-116, 180, 186
bookstore, 167, 176, 197, 220
boomers, 203
bored, 140, 199
born, 16, 79, 103, 138
boundaries, 51, 60, 94, 96, 108, 213
box, 60-61
bragging, 31
brain, 171
brainstorm, 141
brand, 2, 89, 108, 181, 185
Branding, 177, 180-181, 183
branding, 180-181, 183
Brazil, 186
breakthrough, 139
breed, 164
brethren, 4, 45, 110
Brian, 70
brilliant, 207
British, 51
brochure, 182, 197
brochures, 170, 182, 196
brokenhearted, 76
browbeaten, 104
Brunei, 186
budget, 167, 183
bundles, 14, 54
burden, 145
burdened, 132
burdens, 145, 212
buried, 119
Bush, 2, 4, 6, 8, 10, 12, 14, 16, 18, 20, 22, 24, 26, 28-30, 32, 34, 36, 38, 40, 42, 44, 46, 48, 50, 52, 54, 56-58, 60, 62, 64, 66, 68, 70, 72, 74, 76, 78, 80, 82, 84, 86, 88, 90, 92, 94, 96, 98, 100, 102, 104, 106, 108, 110, 112, 114, 116, 118, 120, 122, 124, 126, 128, 130, 132, 134, 136, 138, 140, 142, 144, 146, 148, 150, 152, 154, 156, 158, 160, 162, 164, 166, 168, 170, 172, 174, 176, 178, 180, 182, 184, 186, 188, 190, 192, 194, 196, 198, 200, 202, 204, 206, 208, 210, 212, 214, 216, 218, 220, 222, 224
Business, 27, 163, 168, 176, 181, 191, 202, 213
business, 25, 27-32, 35, 44, 57, 117, 123, 149, 155-156, 159-160, 163-167, 170, 173-177, 179-183, 186, 191, 196-198, 201-203, 206, 211, 215, 219-221
busy, 97, 194, 224

C

calendar, 171
called, 4, 6, 12, 25, 39, 49-50, 78, 80, 104,
123, 131-132, 143-144, 161, 164-165, 174, 205
calling, 4, 26, 39, 57, 77-78, 144, 156, 158, 165, 173-174, 179
calm, 81
Cambodia, 186
Cameroon, 186
Canada, 51, 186
candidates, 202
capabilities, 58, 113
capable, 13, 131, 177, 199
capacity, 160, 222-223
captive, 12

captives, 76
career, 7, 27, 34, 93, 173, 176, 219
Caribbean, 134
catalyst, 117
catalysts, 1
categories, 118, 125, 182
categorize, 87
category, 2, 31, 119
cause, 7, 73, 122, 194
causes, 46, 70, 165
CCLC, 50, 70, 160
celebrate, 37, 85, 120, 134
census, 157
centered, 13, 23, 210
certification, 31, 51, 106, 164, 218
Certified, 29, 50, 62, 103, 176, 220
certified, 16, 50, 161, 178, 193-194
challenges, 23, 50, 59, 79, 102, 124, 130, 156, 202, 206, 212, 224
changing, 13, 33, 37, 66, 71, 176
character, 2, 131, 164, 219
characteristics, 49, 58, 67, 182
charismatic, 57
charismatics, 58
check, 161, 167, 169, 171, 196, 203
cheerleader, 22
choices, 15, 23, 41, 66, 77, 84, 93, 100, 124, 129-130
choose, 35, 70, 146, 161, 175, 214
chosen, 9, 17, 70, 149, 167
Chris, 11, 21, 209
Christ, 4-5, 7-9, 12-13, 23, 25-26, 28, 37, 42-45, 53, 55, 58, 61-62, 70, 76, 78-79, 109, 120, 131-133, 138, 164, 174, 210, 212, 214

CHRISTIAN, 22, 25, 30, 210
christiancoachingweek, 186
Christians, 2-3, 8, 16, 22, 39-40, 43-44, 50, 52-53, 58-59, 62, 67, 71, 81, 88, 97, 119-120, 139, 166, 175, 209
Christy, 29
Church, 84, 176
church, 2, 4, 16, 25, 31, 42, 47, 57, 63, 95, 164-166, 173, 185, 218
churched, 166
churches, 57, 73, 118, 196
circumstances, 11, 67, 82, 94, 129, 131, 147, 152
claim, 13, 16, 30, 134
clarification, 26, 152
clarify, 98, 122, 160
clarity, 76, 78, 81, 97-98, 130, 138, 145, 160
class, 54, 178
classes, 7, 146, 196
classifieds, 184
clear, 16, 19, 22, 39, 43-45, 59, 69, 95-96, 110, 112, 139, 173-174, 187, 212
clergy, 165
client, 5, 13-15, 21-24, 27, 30, 46-47, 52-53, 57, 59, 67-69, 71, 73, 76-81, 83-85, 88-92, 115-116, 118, 121-122, 127-129, 133-135, 137-149, 152-162, 170, 174, 178, 180-183, 187, 192-193, 201-202, 204, 210-211, 214-215
clientele, 221
Clients, 15, 59, 157, 196-197
clients, 5, 7-9, 12, 15, 18, 27-28, 30-31, 34, 45, 47, 50-52, 54, 59, 66-67, 69, 71, 76-77, 79, 82, 84, 88, 90-91, 96, 115-116, 121-122, 125, 127-129, 134,

144-145, 147, 156, 160, 166, 171, 173, 175-176, 178, 180-181, 183, 187-188, 192-193, 195-197, 199-201, 203-205, 211, 213, 217, 219-220, 222
clinical, 68, 217
clinics, 202, 219
COACH, 50, 68, 142
Coachable, 65
coachable, 65, 67, 160
coached, 22, 27, 51, 66, 68, 79, 105, 149, 196, 206
coachee, 124-125
Coaches, 2, 49-50, 53, 87, 89, 117-118, 141, 145, 176
coaches, 1, 4-5, 11-14, 25, 27, 30-31, 37, 44-47, 49-53, 56-57, 59, 61, 64, 66, 69, 71, 73, 75, 80, 84, 87-90, 92, 118, 121, 127-128, 134, 140, 144-145, 151, 155-160, 166-167, 173-176, 178, 181, 186, 191-192, 194, 200-201, 203-204, 207, 209, 212, 214-215, 219, 221
COACHING, 22, 24-25, 59, 65, 91, 167, 210
Coaching, 6, 11, 14-15, 21-23, 26-27, 29-30, 42-43, 45-47, 51, 56, 66, 69, 75, 84-85, 87, 118, 121, 124-126, 130, 141, 151, 159, 161, 176, 185-186, 191, 193, 208, 211, 215, 217, 220-221
collaborate, 141
collaborated, 204
collaboration, 115, 222
collaborative, 22, 79
colleagues, 14, 92
Collins, 27, 58, 118
Colossians, 10, 12

Columbia, 51
comfort, 94, 97
comfortable, 13, 89, 95, 120, 141-142, 151, 206
comforter, 58
commanded, 108
commission, 154
commitment, 10, 80, 129, 152-154, 180, 198, 219-221
committed, 18, 41, 111, 115, 130, 153, 159, 221
communicate, 61-62, 64, 83, 103, 188, 203
communication, 30, 50, 82, 85, 140, 214
communion, 44
community, 69, 148, 165-166, 175, 185-186, 196
company, 102, 185-186, 207
Compassion, 99
compassion, 10, 138, 181
compassionate, 78
compelling, 188, 195, 201
compensate, 201
compete, 157, 221
competencies, 88, 211
competent, 88-89
competitors, 158, 181, 201, 221
complain, 68
compliance, 23, 203
compliant, 203
compliment, 207
complimentary, 161
Comprehensive, 3, 5, 7, 9, 13, 15, 17, 19, 23, 25, 27, 29, 31, 35, 37, 41, 43, 45, 47, 51, 53, 57, 59, 61, 63, 67, 69, 71, 73, 77, 79, 81, 83, 85, 89, 91, 95, 97-99, 103, 105, 109, 111, 113, 115, 119, 121, 123, 125, 129, 131, 133, 135, 139, 141, 143, 145,

147, 149, 153, 157, 159, 161, 165, 167, 169, 171, 173, 175, 179, 181, 183, 185, 187, 189, 193, 195, 197, 201, 203, 205, 207, 211, 213, 215, 219, 221, 223
comprehensive, 163
compromise, 16-17, 47, 100
compromising, 13, 47, 70
computer, 170, 192, 203, 219
conceited, 5, 10
concept, 13, 42, 53, 70, 95
concerns, 175, 199, 203, 212, 221
conclusions, 3, 119
concordance, 37
condemnation, 78, 132
conduct, 87, 209-210
conferences, 7
confesses, 24
confessing, 56, 133
confidence, 29, 81, 85, 89, 99, 111, 118, 132, 145, 161, 173, 194, 215
confident, 29, 50, 77, 83, 121, 157, 215, 224
confidential, 21-22, 92, 210
confidentiality, 69, 210
confidentially, 68
confidently, 30
confirmation, 91, 224
conflict, 52, 67, 94, 96, 211, 215
conflicted, 53, 94-95, 97
conflicts, 15, 52, 210
conformed, 4, 110
confront, 211
confronted, 174, 182
confuse, 45, 182
confused, 45, 210
confusing, 14, 41
confusion, 73
congregations, 57
conquer, 6
conquerors, 131, 133
conscience, 141
consciousness, 90
consecrated, 76
consequential, 122
consequently, 2, 13, 56, 103
consistency, 183
consistent, 110, 173, 181-183
consistently, 111, 149, 207, 213
consortium, 51
consulting, 126, 203
consumer, 115, 182
contemplate, 119, 123
contemporary, 56, 70, 111
context, 13, 34, 37, 107
contingency, 125, 155
contingent, 120
contract, 159, 161, 170, 215
contractual, 44
contradict, 111, 139
contrary, 42, 52-53
convenience, 185
conversation, 62-64, 72, 76, 85, 142, 144-145
conversations, 83, 139
conviction, 79, 178
convictions, 104
convinced, 16, 27, 78
convincing, 57
cooperate, 103
cope, 117, 122
Corinthians, 4-5, 10, 36, 44, 58, 76, 79, 97, 110, 114, 120, 131-133, 138-139
corporations, 126
correction, 71, 211
cost, 102, 176, 180, 192
counsel, 2, 46, 48
Counseling, 6, 14-15, 22, 29, 42, 56, 58, 73, 126, 208, 215, 220

counseling, 21-22, 27, 51-52, 67-70, 72-73, 146, 217-218
Counselor, 218
counselor, 57-58, 68-69, 71, 92, 146, 217-218
Counselors, 73
counselors, 69, 73, 166-167, 176, 215
countenance, 112
counterfeit, 13
couple, 72, 146, 156, 159, 180, 187, 194
courage, 60, 103-104
courageous, 79, 103
course, 13-15, 27-28, 32, 36, 45-46, 54, 71, 88, 102, 104, 111, 141-142, 146, 156, 159-160, 174-176, 220
courses, 12-14, 36, 51, 106, 220
coveting, 97
cowardice, 81
CPLC, 160
creativity, 221
credential, 14
credentialing, 52
credentials, 29, 72, 108, 188
credibility, 30, 100, 178, 180-181
credible, 173
Creed, 57, 210
criteria, 2, 15, 27, 52, 66-67, 111, 200-202
criterion, 42, 52, 161
critical, 12, 75, 96, 157, 203
curriculum, 15

D

darkness, 35, 44, 109, 223
Dave, 29
Day, 203
deadlines, 171
dealing, 26, 117, 122, 145
dealings, 164, 211
Debbie, 173, 176
debriefing, 192
deceit, 12
deceitful, 48
deception, 18, 41, 43, 45
deceptions, 9, 45
decide, 15, 160, 185, 188, 220
decision, 35, 68, 94, 116, 160, 199, 215
dedicated, 62, 121, 179
dedication, 219
deeds, 94, 114, 212
defeat, 13, 31, 43, 112
delay, 13, 29, 36
delays, 39
delegate, 222
denominational, 118
depression, 146
derail, 140
design, 25, 132, 170-171, 180
desire, 2, 5, 15, 18, 57, 72, 76, 91, 94, 101-102, 124, 160, 178, 200-201
despair, 5, 32, 72, 114
destiny, 4, 13, 22, 30, 40, 57, 111, 218, 224
detours, 39-40
Deuteronomy, 79, 132
diagnose, 72
diagram, 24
Dianne, 98, 210
direct, 11, 29, 70, 93, 127, 133, 221
direction, 29, 31, 79, 108, 142, 205, 207, 210, 212, 218, 222
disappoint, 108
disappointed, 60, 120

disbelief, 90
discern, 42, 70-71, 135, 138-139
discerning, 111
discernment, 9, 43, 67, 82, 85, 91, 98, 139, 218
discipline, 6, 9-10, 37, 81, 83, 90, 93, 95, 100, 130
disciplined, 35, 84
discomfort, 139
disconnect, 97
discounted, 134
discourage, 13, 44
discouraged, 104, 132
discouragement, 224
discover, 25, 31, 60, 76-77, 93, 100, 129, 135, 146, 182, 205, 207
discovered, 12, 33, 95, 97, 102, 110
discuss, 63, 69, 96, 103, 118-119, 153, 160
discussion, 22, 64, 128
dishonor, 88-89
disingenuous, 53
disobey, 47
disqualify, 158
disregard, 41, 44, 197
disservice, 100
disturbed, 82
diverse, 54
division, 138
divorce, 145-149
doctor, 198
doctrine, 104
donate, 168
donation, 194
doves, 143-144
Dr, 56-57, 176, 210
dream, 101, 110, 145
dreams, 23, 28, 95, 146
drudgery, 104
duties, 9, 70, 222-223
Duty, 29, 144
duty, 7, 34, 90, 104-105, 144, 210

E

eagles, 83
earnest, 80, 133
earnestly, 77
earning, 191
earnings, 204
ears, 9, 17, 90
earth, 16, 56, 58, 62, 94, 97, 108, 115, 175
earthly, 111
easy, 37, 154, 166, 192, 201, 206, 219
eBook, 147, 183, 188, 197, 204
eBooks, 180, 182
Ecclesiastes, 5, 17, 28, 84
economic, 120, 218
educate, 178
educated, 12-13, 26
education, 7, 50, 62, 149, 182, 220
educator, 57
effective, 14, 22, 79, 115, 117, 140, 185, 217-218
efficient, 156, 191
effort, 66, 140, 215
ego, 90
elevate, 7
emanate, 24
embarrassed, 200
embrace, 97, 119, 121-122
Emery, 51
Emory, 14
emotional, 22, 123, 180, 182-183
emotionally, 102, 146

emotions, 58, 140, 142, 146, 149
employment, 102, 207, 219
empowered, 93, 112
enable, 180
encourage, 12, 25-26, 29, 59, 133, 146-149, 164, 175, 185, 213, 218
encouraged, 41, 52, 91, 131
encouragement, 22, 146
encourages, 23, 36, 52, 61
endeavors, 111
enhance, 62, 115, 180, 212
enjoy, 37, 67, 159, 194, 207
enormous, 206
enough, 12, 29, 43, 60, 66, 70, 72, 89-90, 97, 109, 119, 128, 155, 166, 174, 200-202, 223
enrich, 25
enrollees, 43
enrolling, 51, 54
enrollment, 12
enthusiasm, 129
enthusiastic, 103
enthusiastically, 17
entitled, 4, 14, 70, 147, 159
entrepreneur, 30, 221
entrepreneurs, 176
environment, 176
environmental, 23
environments, 83-85
envision, 142, 145, 174
Ephesians, 28, 78, 83
epistle, 4
equipment, 170, 180
essential, 6, 100, 145, 176
eternal, 130
ethical, 41, 175, 209, 213
ethics, 67, 169, 211, 215
Ethiopia, 186
Evan, 29, 60-61
evangelism, 164

evidence, 89, 195
evil, 10, 44, 63, 82, 94, 109, 175
examine, 8, 59, 66, 100
example, 3, 12, 40, 63, 94, 97, 103, 112, 115, 118, 123, 143-144, 147, 182-183, 186, 201, 203-204, 206, 221
exceedingly, 28
excellence, 4, 7, 10, 23, 35, 53, 70, 77, 85, 88-89, 94, 145, 173, 211, 218, 220
excellent, 3-4, 7, 35, 83, 137, 146, 157, 176, 178-180, 192
excited, 27, 104, 120-121, 206
excitement, 112
excuse, 161
execute, 125, 179, 224
execution, 30, 123, 125-126
exhausted, 96, 112
exhilarating, 160
exhort, 59, 166
exhortation, 22, 26
expect, 34, 43, 52, 80, 83, 109, 157, 173
expectation, 109
expenses, 219
expensive, 215
experiences, 26, 72, 131, 203, 223
expert, 179, 188, 201, 206
expertise, 30, 69, 88, 178, 192, 206
extraordinary, 139, 157-158
eye, 35, 212
eyes, 61, 76, 103, 105, 142, 197

F

face, 43, 94, 133, 174
Facebook, 184
facilitate, 30

facilitator, 157
faculty, 51
failure, 104, 124, 130
fair, 115, 143
fairly, 109, 157, 203, 214
Faith, 55, 99
faith, 5, 7, 11-12, 16-17, 27, 30, 42, 45, 47, 49, 52-53, 60-61, 64, 67, 70, 77-79, 89-91, 95, 103, 113-115, 120-121, 124, 132-133, 144, 147-148, 180, 210
faithbased, 13
faithful, 5, 18, 114, 143, 175, 197
faithfulness, 77
false, 3, 130, 174
Father, 25, 32, 44, 58, 94, 108, 133, 138
father, 17-18, 97
fear, 5, 17, 34, 79, 81, 84-85, 90-91, 111, 119-120, 124, 129, 134, 139, 141, 148, 174, 214, 221
fearful, 223
fears, 90, 124
feeling, 19, 28, 36, 140-141, 143, 157, 188
feelings, 12, 23, 58, 72, 122
fellowship, 44, 76, 84, 109, 165
fictions, 9, 16-17, 45
fight, 79, 120, 124
finances, 130, 160, 202, 208
fish, 6, 27, 147
flawed, 12, 110
flesh, 31, 79, 94, 132
Florida, 186, 211
Florine, 56
follow, 31, 35, 41, 68, 78, 88, 91, 97-98, 142, 151, 167, 192, 204
follower, 42
followers, 41, 43, 76, 94, 184, 214

fool, 18
foolish, 124, 131
forgive, 10
formula, 109, 156, 192, 204
forsaken, 114
fortunate, 2, 46, 48, 108
forum, 220
foundation, 10, 16-17, 23, 40, 46, 55, 75, 160, 220, 223
foundational, 40, 52, 55
founder, 4
Free, 87-88, 104, 210
free, 42, 53, 78, 83, 97-98, 133-134, 144, 151, 156, 173, 175, 180, 184-185, 188, 192, 196, 220-221
freedom, 151
fruit, 3, 83, 112
fruition, 114
fruitless, 133
fruits, 3
frustrate, 112
frustrated, 31, 40, 53, 96, 112, 173
fueled, 174
fullness, 96, 109, 114
fun, 106, 134, 207
future, 21, 101, 112, 120-121, 124, 139, 145, 147, 189

G

gained, 30, 51, 89, 130
Galatians, 42, 145, 212
Gary, 27, 58, 118
general, 21, 26, 63, 109, 112, 151-152, 203
generalist, 206
generations, 56
gentleness, 212
genuine, 53, 93

Ghost, 25, 57
ghost, 169
gift, 26, 78, 133-134, 139, 166, 224
gifted, 71, 166, 197, 206
gifts, 6, 23, 76-77, 110, 113-114, 139, 156, 173, 193, 197, 218, 223
gimmick, 200
global, 41
glorify, 94
glory, 29-30, 113, 131
gluttony, 36
goal, 3, 5, 27, 30, 35, 47, 69, 84, 89, 105,
111, 113, 115, 118, 122, 125, 134, 139, 149, 152-154, 157-159, 184, 188-189, 202, 210-211
goals, 12, 21-24, 52, 75, 78, 82, 84, 108, 115,
118, 134, 146, 148-149, 156, 160, 176,
193, 212, 220
GOD, 56, 60
godless, 15-16, 45
godliness, 4, 16, 41, 45
Google, 184, 195
Gospel, 42, 76
govern, 209
grace, 7, 31, 42, 78, 83, 85, 94, 111-112, 131, 133-134, 147, 179-180
graduate, 221
graphic, 171, 180
grateful, 132
Greek, 42
Grief, 176
grief, 58, 146, 176
griefcoachingcenter, 176
groups, 17, 30, 156-157, 196, 206-207, 220-221
growth, 105, 120, 207, 219-220
guard, 79, 138
guidance, 152-153, 206, 214, 218, 222
guilt, 58, 72
guilty, 18, 78, 166
Guinea, 186

H

Habakkuk, 109
happy, 2, 8, 11, 26, 82, 94-95, 108
hardship, 133
harmful, 211
harmonious, 82
harmony, 24, 132
haughtily, 10
haughtiness, 37
haughty, 112
headlines, 188
headquarters, 164
headshot, 187
healed, 61
healing, 22, 97, 146
health, 35, 71-72, 123, 202-203, 217, 219
healthy, 21-22, 35, 73, 125, 146
heart, 18-19, 24, 31, 50, 77, 82, 90, 95, 113, 125, 132, 145-147, 149, 194, 212
heaven, 32, 42, 94, 108
Heavenly, 133
heavenly, 171
Hebrews, 5, 59, 77, 83, 89, 133, 212
Heisman, 105
Helpers, 58
Hezekiah, 79
Hilton, 14, 51
hiring, 80, 171, 187, 219

history, 95, 104
holiness, 164
homework, 159
honesty, 95, 215
honored, 138
hope, 5, 28, 60, 76, 83, 91, 101, 103, 109, 120, 143, 147-148, 218
html, 188, 195
human, 12-13, 23, 131
humanism, 40
humanistic, 13, 41
humanists, 16
humble, 31, 36, 111-112
humility, 10
husband, 29, 34, 60-61, 71, 102-103
Hypnosis, 46
hypnosis, 13, 41
hypocrites, 114

I

IBM, 178
idle, 12, 44, 213
idleness, 44
idolatry, 18, 36, 46
idols, 44
illegal, 211
implement, 98, 167, 218
improve, 15, 17, 65, 73, 92, 121, 162, 218
improvement, 2, 7, 66, 91, 159, 167, 169-170
improvisation, 125
impure, 16, 45
inaccurate, 43
incompatible, 13, 53
increase, 41, 50, 72, 83, 138, 154, 157, 178-179, 181, 197, 223

India, 186
industry, 15, 17, 51, 88, 105, 192, 200-203, 209, 219
infidel, 44
infirmities, 131
Influence, 99
influence, 3, 5-6, 100
influential, 5, 100, 131
Ingram, 105
injustice, 10
inklings, 50, 139
inquiry, 12, 158
inspiration, 97
inspirational, 83
inspire, 112, 120, 135, 139, 143
instinct, 139
instruction, 9, 17, 45
instructions, 2, 45, 90
intake, 69, 160, 162
integrity, 10, 50, 100, 164, 211, 215
intellectualism, 12
intelligent, 141-142
intense, 194
intentions, 12
interpersonal, 81
interpretation, 8, 120
interpretations, 139
interrupt, 140-141
intersecting, 24
interview, 11
intimacy, 138
intimidating, 121
intolerable, 96, 105
intuition, 139
intuitive, 149, 193, 201
Iron, 112
iron, 112, 209
irrational, 130, 140
irrelevant, 119, 158
irreverent, 16, 45

irritability, 72
Isaiah, 76, 83, 110, 118, 120
Israelites, 107

J

James, 19, 114, 138
January, 203
Jehovah, 166
Jenny, 205, 208
jennygracemorris, 208
Jeremiah, 40, 101, 109, 147, 165
Jews, 4, 62
Jirah, 166
Job, 123
John, 16, 42-43, 58, 63, 80, 91, 109, 132
Joseph, 110
journaling, 146
journey, 36, 56, 113, 220
joy, 5, 18, 58, 83, 90, 112, 114, 144, 147, 175-176
Judah, 79
judge, 41, 214
judgment, 2, 78, 94
judgmental, 23, 50, 212
Juliet, 4

K

Kathy, 145, 149
key, 64, 125, 156, 195, 205
keywords, 195
kind, 10, 41, 53, 78, 125, 144, 213
King, 71
king, 79, 165
Kingdom, 34, 53-54, 111, 164, 166, 186, 197
kingdom, 3, 23, 32, 48, 56, 82, 111, 175
kingly, 165
KJV, 2-3, 42, 44, 77, 89, 91, 110, 114, 118, 120, 131-133
Koch, 70

L

lamp, 35, 94
land, 77, 132, 154
language, 82
launching, 198
law, 2, 62, 79, 108, 210, 212, 215
lawyer, 124, 198
lay, 45, 218
lazy, 175, 223
leader, 15, 17, 100
leaders, 2, 37, 53, 100, 119, 201
Leadership, 6-7
leadership, 2, 5-6, 100, 115, 214
learning, 7, 36, 50, 80, 82, 125, 131, 179, 220-221, 223
Leelo, 2, 4, 6, 8, 10, 12, 14, 16, 18, 20, 22, 24, 26, 28, 30, 32, 34, 36, 38, 40, 42, 44, 46, 48, 50, 52, 54, 56, 58, 60, 62, 64, 66, 68, 70, 72, 74, 76, 78, 80, 82, 84, 86, 88, 90, 92, 94, 96, 98, 100, 102, 104, 106, 108, 110, 112, 114, 116, 118, 120, 122, 124, 126, 128, 130, 132, 134, 136, 138, 140, 142, 144, 146, 148, 150, 152, 154, 156, 158, 160, 162, 164, 166, 168, 170, 172, 174, 176, 178, 180, 182, 184, 186, 188, 190, 192, 194, 196, 198, 200, 202, 204, 206, 208, 210, 212, 214, 216, 218, 220, 222, 224
leelobush, 221
Legacy, 99

legal, 51, 175
legally, 174, 215
Leshinsky, 204
liability, 170, 215
liberating, 60
liberty, 76
license, 51
licenses, 167
licensing, 167
lifestyle, 41, 52, 95, 149, 203
lifestyles, 23, 95
lifetime, 6, 27, 61, 193
limit, 133, 200
limitations, 23, 61, 70
Linguistic, 46
LinkedIn, 184
Listening, 137-138, 145
listening, 50, 70, 90, 109,
    137-138, 140, 144, 178, 206
litigation, 51
litigious, 215
local, 169, 175, 178, 185-187, 191,
    196-197
logical, 59, 151, 205
logistical, 123
loss, 60, 124, 145, 176, 210
Love, 10, 36, 64, 99, 183
loyalty, 180
Luke, 2, 9, 48, 57, 70, 78, 132,
    164, 179
Lutheran, 57

M

magnitude, 201
majority, 217, 224
manage, 45, 92, 209
management, 26, 96, 99, 167,
    171, 192, 204
manifest, 28
manifested, 92, 114

manipulation, 13, 46
mankind, 16
Mark, 105
marketable, 27
Marketing, 28, 45, 177-179,
    183, 192
Marketplace, 30
marketplace, 44-45, 164-165,
    197
marriage, 44, 102, 159, 207
Marshall, 164-165
Martha, 70
Mary, 70
Master, 10, 29, 56, 61, 79, 123,
    126, 145, 149, 173, 176, 205,
    208, 220
masterminds, 220-221
masters, 48, 52
Matthew, 3, 5, 18, 23, 32, 35, 44,
    48, 50, 54, 56, 62, 77, 82,
    94, 97, 108, 111, 114, 132, 197,
    211, 222-223
mature, 8, 120
maturity, 2-3, 47
mavericks, 120
May, 57, 76
MCLC, 63, 123, 145, 173, 205
meaning, 24, 43, 45, 62, 66, 148
measurable, 66, 68
media, 176, 184-185, 196,
    219-220
meditation, 82
meetup, 185
men, 12, 17, 42, 62, 79, 83-84,
    94-95, 132, 206
mental, 22, 34, 71-72, 112, 171,
    175, 217, 219
mentality, 67
Mentor, 221
mentor, 79, 130, 172, 221
mentoring, 172

mentors, 176
mercies, 110
mercy, 92, 94, 131, 133, 147
Merriam, 40-41
Message, 10
Messiah, 12, 212
method, 88, 90-92, 153-154
methodology, 3
methods, 13, 60, 83, 88, 90, 115, 158
Microsoft, 171, 192
Milana, 204
military, 103
millennium, 203
Miller, 61, 63, 123, 126
Milligan, 56
mindful, 35, 37
minister, 45, 165
ministers, 44, 164-165
ministries, 167
ministry, 1, 25, 77, 156, 164-165, 173-174, 177, 186, 197, 218
miracles, 34, 61, 164
misconduct, 212
mission, 11, 62, 104, 115-116, 144, 164, 167, 181
missionaries, 4
mistakes, 66, 94, 183, 221
mockers, 2, 46, 48
model, 3, 36, 59, 87, 92, 130, 179
Moishe, 4
momentum, 134
money, 14, 31, 48, 90, 105, 134, 160, 164, 174, 191, 197
mood, 149
moral, 2, 41, 94, 164, 212
morally, 3, 53
morals, 23, 67
mother, 57, 60, 97, 148
motivate, 180-181
motivated, 91, 134, 178, 188
motivation, 5, 31, 77, 88, 111, 129
Mount, 94
Mt, 4
mtjuliet, 4
Murphy, 125
Muslim, 63
Myanmar, 186
Myers, 211
myth, 29
myths, 9, 16-17, 45

N

Namibia, 186
Narrow, 1
nature, 84, 112, 222
negative, 120, 134, 149, 224
neglect, 9, 60, 144
negotiate, 161
negotiating, 160
neighbor, 64, 97
nervousness, 34
Neuro, 46
newage, 3
newsletter, 188, 196
newspaper, 185
newsworthy, 196
niche, 14, 88, 149, 167, 173, 180-183, 185, 191-192, 197, 199-208
niches, 14, 121
Nigeria, 186
NIV, 70, 131-133, 209, 212-213
NKJV, 62
NLP, 13, 46
noble, 94, 116, 131
Nonbelievers, 134
nonsense, 12
normal, 62

novice, 66, 155, 157
nudges, 142-144
nullify, 131

O

obedience, 61, 67, 114, 212, 214
obedient, 92, 144
obey, 83
objections, 178
objective, 124, 152, 195
objectivity, 130
obligation, 139, 211
obstacle, 129, 132, 134, 143, 173, 207
obstacles, 23, 26, 70, 114, 127, 129-132, 153-154
offended, 11-12, 72
offense, 10
office, 29, 144, 169-170, 191-192, 198, 219
Omega, 92
online, 182, 186
operate, 116, 219
optimist, 60
optimum, 30, 88, 156
ordained, 26
ordinances, 169
ordination, 51
organic, 112
organized, 25-26, 83, 88, 164, 184
Oswald, 6
outcome, 3, 24, 47, 67-68, 109, 113, 115, 121, 123, 130, 152-154, 214
outcomes, 22, 103, 113
Outlook, 171, 192
overcome, 26, 50, 73, 127, 130-132, 153-154, 178
overcomer, 67

overwhelmed, 130, 147
overwhelming, 102, 147, 153
ownership, 57, 175

P

PA, 70
pain, 144
painful, 83
panacea, 45
pantheism, 41
Parable, 18, 50, 197, 223
parable, 175, 223
Paradigm, 3
paradigm, 3, 7-8, 77, 123
paralyze, 68
parameters, 119
Paraphrased, 9, 36
paraphrased, 53, 70
Paris, 193
passion, 25, 40, 44, 57, 100-101, 103-106, 144, 174, 201, 207
passionate, 103-105, 139, 148, 164, 206-207
passions, 101, 103, 113, 116, 173
Pastor, 70
pastor, 56-57, 112
pastoral, 164
pastors, 1, 118
patient, 10, 36, 73, 156, 198, 213
patriotism, 41
payment, 160
PayPal, 188
PCCCA, 42, 50, 61-62, 103, 126, 176, 179, 197, 207-208, 218, 221
peace, 29, 96-97, 109, 138, 144, 213
Peer, 15, 51-52
pendulum, 218

perfect, 12, 15, 29, 91-92, 94, 110, 130-131, 211
Periscope, 184
permission, 29, 76, 92, 153-154, 215
persecuted, 114
persecution, 133
persistence, 219
personalized, 112, 161, 205
persuasive, 100
persuasiveness, 82
Peter, 31, 82-83, 111, 214
PhD, 118
Philippians, 4-5, 78, 132, 138
philosophies, 9, 12-13, 15, 39, 59
philosophy, 12-13, 27, 40-41, 187
phobia, 130
phone, 11, 17, 52, 72, 143, 158, 169-171, 179, 186, 191, 215, 219
phonies, 114
physical, 34-35, 45, 76, 202
physician, 156
physiological, 96
Picasso, 193
Pinterest, 184
pipeline, 192
planning, 7, 60, 125, 142, 163, 175-176, 222-223
positive, 47, 50, 57, 73, 113, 117, 144, 207, 219
possess, 25, 36, 104, 137, 173
possibilities, 103, 105
potential, 51, 77, 140, 177, 222
poverty, 60
power, 2, 5, 16-17, 24, 55, 57, 61, 79, 81, 83, 92, 108, 114-115, 124, 131-133, 147, 180, 211, 214, 217

powerful, 13, 50, 57, 89, 92, 97, 127, 217
practical, 8, 14, 50, 53, 151, 164-165, 201
practicum, 51, 66
practitioner, 174
praise, 94
praiseworthy, 94
pray, 7, 9, 33-34, 40, 64, 113, 133, 139, 147, 179-180, 205, 220
prayer, 23-24, 109, 125, 132, 138, 152-154, 214
preach, 76
preachers, 4, 57
preaching, 164
predetermined, 104
predictable, 151, 155-156, 203
prejudice, 140
Presbyterian, 57
prescribe, 156
prescribed, 109
presentation, 134
presentations, 134, 182
president, 15, 29, 51
presumptuous, 31, 111, 193
pricing, 115
principles, 23, 47, 209
print, 184-185
priorities, 3, 82, 85, 93, 112, 115, 162, 222
prioritize, 94, 98
prioritized, 222
priority, 47, 111, 162
prison, 76
proactive, 117
proactively, 96
proceed, 19, 47, 67, 141, 153, 160
product, 3, 15, 30, 80, 87, 178, 182-183, 204-205
productive, 117, 128, 156, 173

profanity, 17
Professional, 6, 14-15, 29, 42, 71, 126, 159, 208, 215, 217, 220
professionally, 51, 53, 186-187, 211, 213
Proficiencies, 75, 85
proficiencies, 23, 75-76, 180, 217-218
proficiency, 44, 76
profit, 165
promote, 18, 30, 35, 45, 52, 111, 177, 185, 192
promotion, 27, 132, 183, 220
propaganda, 16
prophesied, 17, 32
prophets, 3
prospect, 27, 182-183, 204, 222
prospects, 181-182
prosper, 3, 101, 147
prosperous, 2, 46, 48
protocol, 215
Proverb, 125
Proverbs, 9, 44, 81-82, 107-108, 111-112, 132, 138, 209
Psalm, 3, 77, 81-82
psalm, 46
Psalms, 46, 48
pulpit, 165
purpose, 4, 10, 23, 26, 57, 62, 73, 81, 83, 85, 100-101, 107-109, 112, 114, 116, 120, 123, 132, 148, 165-166, 186, 204, 210

Q

quality, 6, 8, 14-15, 52, 83, 94, 183

question, 16, 39, 41, 43, 56, 69-70, 105, 128-129, 160, 162, 174, 183, 204, 206, 222
quiet, 10, 139, 143, 160, 194
quiz, 188
quote, 4, 62

R

radical, 57
radically, 13, 120
raise, 40, 78, 153-154, 193
Ramsey, 29
rapport, 159, 161
rational, 15, 59
rationale, 43
reactions, 118
realistic, 15
reality, 12, 44, 117-118, 125, 178
reciprocal, 184, 196
recommend, 11, 64, 69, 73, 97, 151, 158, 171-172, 180, 185, 197, 220
recommendation, 52, 69, 176
records, 170
recovery, 145-146
recurring, 205
Reddit, 184
redeem, 147
Redeemer, 82
redemptive, 108
referral, 69, 71-73, 158, 196
referrals, 73, 198, 219
regimen, 69, 220
registrations, 167
regulated, 212
reinforce, 134, 181, 214
rejoice, 10, 138
relate, 203, 206, 221
relationships, 21, 58, 73, 95-96, 104, 202, 207-208, 212, 214

relativism, 41
relativists, 41
relax, 2, 46, 48
relevance, 58, 138
relevant, 61, 181, 184
reliable, 205
religion, 41-42
reluctant, 121, 153-154, 221
remedies, 156
report, 118, 188
representative, 40
reprimanded, 175
reputation, 2
research, 60, 184
resentful, 10
reserved, 30
residual, 205
Resources, 15, 51-52, 152, 154
resources, 15, 24, 28-29, 34, 83, 92, 153, 166, 175, 187, 196-197, 201, 216, 220-221, 223-224
respect, 26, 35, 69, 140, 144-145, 161, 181, 213, 215
respecter, 214
responsibility, 2, 7, 68, 144, 173
responsible, 24, 149
responsive, 212
Restoration, 176
restored, 62, 94
result, 96, 113, 141, 157, 187, 205
Rev, 77, 210
Revelations, 45, 165
revelations, 82, 91
reverential, 214
revival, 57
reward, 134
rewarder, 77
Rey, 15, 51
rhema, 57
Rich, 164
richer, 67, 117
risk, 68, 88-90, 103, 106, 125, 130, 175, 201
ritual, 222
road, 35-36, 42, 164
Romans, 4, 58, 79, 94, 110, 123, 132-133, 212, 214
romantic, 36, 103
Rosen, 4
RSS, 184
rudimentary, 12
rules, 41, 105, 210, 214

S

sabotage, 130
sacrifice, 110, 129
safe, 81, 111, 221
safety, 105
saints, 132
sales, 30, 134, 154, 178, 204, 222
salt, 62-64, 94
saltiness, 62, 94
salty, 62-64
Salvation, 81
salvation, 16, 42, 78, 141
sample, 155, 157-158, 160-161, 167
Sanders, 6
Satan, 13, 23, 43-44, 111, 224
Savior, 26, 42, 44, 55, 210
savvy, 180
scared, 29, 124
scary, 12, 106, 118, 120-121
schedule, 160, 192
scriptural, 13, 130
scripturally, 17, 43, 111
Scripture, 44, 55-56, 101, 109, 114

scripture, 2-3, 13, 25, 28, 31, 42, 44, 46, 55-56, 61-64, 97, 108, 111-112, 123, 128, 159, 175, 211, 214, 223
scriptures, 22, 75, 97, 132, 209, 212
Secular, 12, 23, 40, 53, 59
secular, 3, 13-14, 16-17, 23-25, 40, 43-45, 47, 52, 57, 63, 89, 111
secularists, 41, 139
security, 170-171
selfish, 37
selfless, 36
selling, 158, 178
semantics, 211
seminars, 7, 207
Sermon, 94
serpents, 143-144
servant, 5, 18, 50, 114, 175, 197, 223
servants, 175
serve, 7-8, 18, 36-37, 48, 52, 104, 115, 164-166, 201-202, 220
service, 27, 69, 110, 182-183, 185, 192-193, 201, 204-205, 219
settle, 4, 43-44, 70, 119
sheep, 3
shepherd, 164
shift, 8, 149
signs, 26, 71-72, 97
silence, 108, 143
silent, 160
silly, 16, 45
simple, 33, 63, 131, 194, 204, 206, 219
simplification, 156
simplybeautifulmedia, 171
sin, 36, 58, 79, 109, 212, 214

skill, 222
sleep, 44, 72
slim, 66
SLM, 179-180
slm, 28, 45
sloppy, 35
slothful, 76
sluggish, 5
snakes, 132
Snapchat, 184
Social, 184
social, 100, 176, 184, 219-220
society, 36, 120, 215
Son, 4, 25, 58, 108-109
souls, 35, 143
source, 15, 52, 73, 77, 195, 205
sources, 30, 73, 197
speak, 7, 17, 34, 47, 49, 61, 68, 71, 95, 114, 133, 138, 140, 144, 159-160, 196, 211
speaker, 83
specialist, 102-103
specialize, 204, 206
specialties, 54, 121, 221
specialty, 88, 199-201, 221
speech, 82
Spirit, 4, 9, 13, 19, 24-25, 28-29, 31, 33-35, 40, 42-43, 45-46, 56-59, 64, 67, 71, 76, 79, 88-92, 108, 110-111, 113, 132, 138-139, 142-145, 151-153, 156, 179, 194, 211-212, 214, 217-218
spirit, 5, 9, 78, 81, 110, 124, 144
Spiritual, 6, 77
spiritual, 12, 35-36, 45, 47, 57, 61, 73, 76, 78, 83-84, 164, 173, 212-213
spiritually, 16, 45
spontaneity, 156
stability, 49, 181
stage, 146, 217

stagnate, 88-89
standardizing, 75
standards, 14, 59, 75, 78, 80, 96, 131, 209-210, 212-213
Stankovich, 173, 176
steward, 45
stewardship, 175
story, 17, 70, 92, 102-103, 142, 174, 193
Strasberg, 206
strategic, 44, 188, 223
strategies, 9, 45, 48, 91, 130, 134, 154, 160, 180, 183, 218
strategize, 22, 141
strength, 10, 19, 79, 83, 94, 98, 114, 131, 133, 143
success, 3-4, 7, 23, 26, 31-32, 66, 77, 85, 102, 104, 124, 130, 171, 204, 219
successful, 16, 28, 57, 65-66, 70, 103, 105, 165, 171, 180, 193, 201, 206, 221
suffer, 44, 82, 138
superficial, 53
superior, 41, 68, 213
supervise, 17
supplication, 132, 138
surrender, 110
surveys, 173
survive, 165
suspicions, 129
Switzerland, 186
sword, 43, 97, 133
symptoms, 96
synergy, 156-157
systems, 53, 88, 90, 158

T

tactics, 221
tagline, 182
talent, 166, 173, 175, 206, 223
tax, 167, 169
teaching, 3, 7, 42, 109, 164, 207, 210
tech, 180
technical, 180
technique, 5, 102
techniques, 69, 213, 217-218
technological, 186, 219
technology, 179
tedious, 8
television, 17, 35
template, 185, 205
temple, 35, 44
tempt, 100
terms, 44, 47, 61, 78, 88, 200, 207, 215
Testament, 23
testimonials, 188, 195-196, 205
testimonies, 34, 131
testimony, 26, 49, 58, 92
thanksgiving, 138
thefreedictionary, 36, 88
theologians, 36
theory, 3, 61
therapist, 68-69
Therapists, 73
therapists, 69, 202
Therapy, 22
therapy, 21-22, 67, 69, 72
Thessalonians, 4, 213
thinking, 3, 60-61, 66, 71, 77, 104, 130, 192
thoughts, 12-13, 64, 72, 76, 80, 83, 98, 109-110, 130, 140, 142, 184, 215
Timothy, 2, 5, 7, 9, 16-17, 45, 81, 124
Todd, 61-64, 123, 126
tolerate, 9, 17, 119
tolerations, 23

train, 28, 45
trained, 31, 34, 51, 66, 72, 83, 90, 174
trainer, 14, 53, 61
Training, 13, 49, 52-53, 178
transference, 175
transform, 61
transformation, 66, 96
transformations, 51
transformed, 110-111
transition, 121, 139, 145-149, 219
transitions, 121, 145, 147, 149, 203
trickery, 46
Trinity, 25
Truth, 7, 9, 14, 16, 51, 99, 125, 199
truths, 45, 207

U

ultimate, 92, 113, 166
unaffordable, 172
unaware, 58
unbeliever, 44
unbiased, 51
unbiblical, 13
uncoachable, 67
Uncompromised, 199
unfair, 143
Unforgivable, 147
ungodly, 2, 13, 15, 18, 46, 48
United, 36, 103, 186
universal, 14, 41-42
Universalists, 41
universe, 12
unkempt, 35
unlearn, 121
unlimited, 208
unpretentious, 112
unrighteousness, 44
unscriptural, 13
unwholesome, 82
unwilling, 41, 68, 88-89, 118
update, 114, 176, 187
UPS, 170

V

valid, 12, 26, 110, 122
validate, 17, 51
valuable, 30, 175, 204
Values, 93, 95-99
variables, 109
venture, 202, 222
verse, 3-4, 46, 62-63, 108, 124
vessel, 71
veteran, 204
viability, 122
victim, 67
victory, 224
violence, 17
VIP, 221
virtual, 182, 191, 219, 221
visibility, 179, 185, 222
visions, 28, 77, 82, 110
visitors, 188-189, 195
vocation, 220

W

wardrobe, 10
waste, 67, 187
watching, 17, 119
weak, 62, 131, 211, 213
weakness, 131-132
weary, 83, 104, 132
web, 171, 178, 184, 186, 195-196
webmaster, 195
website, 4, 11, 41, 52, 171, 180, 182, 184, 186-189, 195-196, 204-205, 208, 220

Webster, 40-41
wife, 57
wikipedia, 41
wilderness, 120
willing, 15, 26, 28, 30, 35-36, 56, 61, 65-66, 68, 70, 89, 105, 133, 154, 159, 183, 185, 196-197, 200, 204, 219
willingness, 89
win, 61-62, 125, 161, 205, 222
wisdom, 19, 46, 50, 64, 78, 91, 95, 98, 113, 139, 141, 152-153, 222
witness, 70, 175
witnessed, 61, 90
woman, 53, 96, 103, 105, 146, 148, 193, 206
works, 2, 4, 23-24, 31-33, 43, 63, 72, 77, 114, 118, 141, 156, 158, 179
worldly, 7, 40
worldview, 59, 73, 161
worldviews, 39, 59
worry, 18, 63, 90, 109, 111, 194
Worship, 99
worship, 17, 84
worthy, 45, 51, 97, 112, 115
Wright, 29
write, 6, 8, 10, 39, 42, 112-113, 146, 148, 180
writer, 83
written, 14, 92, 147

www.ingramcontent.com/pod-product-compliance
Lightning Source LLC
Chambersburg PA
CBHW070240230426
43664CB00014B/2370